The Constitution is a ~~Law~~ Contract

Michael DeLance Thomas

www.michaeldelancethomas.com

Harry Tubman Publishing

The Constitution is a ~~Law~~ Contract

Published in the United States by Harry Tubman Publishing

Print ISBN: 978-0-9850288-1-7

Ebook ISBN: 978-0-9850288-2-4

Website: www.michaeldelancethomas.com

Email: support@michaeldelancethomas.com

Book cover design: Arrowdesigns

Editors: Pat Stainke, Dr. Neal Blaxberg, Field Searcy

Printed in the United States of America

Marlen David Thomas
Thank you for your patience. I love you.

Thank you to all those who are fighting for "true" liberty!

Contents

Introduction

The Constitution of the United States of America - is it a law or a contract? Constitutional lawyers, judges, politicians, political scientists, and others purport that it is a law. This position would make sense, considering Article VI of the Constitution mentions that the Constitution of the United States is the "supreme Law of the Land." On the contrary, I purport that the Constitution serves as a political contract and is not a law in the conventional definition and application of the word.

Like many, I grew up believing that the Constitution of the United States was the "Law of the Land." I had no reason to question this general belief until I started studying the history of American government, natural law, the Declaration of Independence, the Articles of Confederation, and the U.S. Constitution. I was excited about this new revelation of the Constitution being a contract but did not initially understand why it mattered in a practical sense. After all, the U.S. Constitution is over two hundred and thirty years old! I asked myself, "What difference would it make if I could prove that it was a contract? Would anyone care? How would it influence the political landscape?" There is truth in the adage that asserts that our perceptions are our reality. If that is true, it goes without saying that our perceptions influence our actions and that our actions determine our future outcomes. Therefore, viewing the Constitution as a contract may have huge ramifications in the political world.

We do ourselves a disservice when we reference the Constitution as a law because it prevents us from understanding the underlying governing framework of the United States as a whole. Furthermore, if our core understanding of something is based on a faulty foundation, then the likelihood that everything that sprouts from that foundation will also be wrong. Similarly, if our underlying understanding of the Constitution is wrong, then many things discussed, written, or adjudicated based on this misunderstanding will be wrong. There is no question that the way we view the Constitution influences the political direction of the United States, either towards liberty or towards bondage. Our natural liberties continue to decline because we have interpreted the Constitution as being a law rather than a contract.

Why Is It important

One aim of this treatise is to offer evidence that the Constitution, itself, is a contract, not a law. But why is this important? Well, if the Constitution is a contract rather than a law, then it begs the question, "What other things do we have wrong?" Perhaps we may not even understand our system of government as we have assumed. Identifying the Constitution as a contract will change how we view its overall purpose and its application to past and future political controversies. This new understanding will also clarify and redefine the *proper* relationship between the federal government and the States. It will reveal how the federal government is overstepping its boundaries and usurping the authority of the States which, in turn, usurps the authority of U.S. citizens. A proper perspective will reveal the correct political relationship between the fifty states, which will have a tremendous impact on current and future political policies. Identifying the Constitution as a contract is also a critical step towards:

- restoring our natural liberties (inalienable rights).
- redistributing political power back to us, as in "We the People".
- reducing the centralization of power within the federal government.
- restoring independence and sovereignty to the States.
- identifying the accurate source of the Constitution's authority.
- securing the Constitution's integrity for future generations.
- exposing how far we have drifted away from the Framers' intentions.
- influencing how we interpret the Constitution's Articles and Amendments.
- reestablishing the idea of a Republican form of government, as the Framers intended, rather than a Democracy.

These are just a few examples of what can be achieved by adopting a correct perspective of the Constitution and its intended purpose. In addition, enforcement of the Constitution is essential in protecting our liberties from being infringed upon by the various governments. A misunderstanding of its purpose diminishes its importance, thus weakening its inherent protections. It stands to reason that anyone who cares about protecting their unalienable rights and liberties should learn the true purpose of the Constitution. It should also be readily appreciated that arriving at this understanding does not require a political science or law degree; rather, all one needs is a genuine interest, an open mind, and the ability to comprehend some fundamental principles. When you finish this book, I strongly encourage you to re-read the Constitution from the perspective of it being a political contract rather than a supreme Law that governs over the populace. The Constitution is a beautiful and important document, but only when correctly understood and applied in its proper context.

Leaving "Law" to Lawyers

We are taught from an early age that the Constitution is a law, which probably explains why so many citizens leave its interpretation and political application to lawyers, lawmakers, politicians, and judges. Interpreting law is not the most appealing task, and most citizens are not interested in delving into Constitutional "law" and its legal mumbo-jumbo; thus, we seem to leave law to lawyers. This is unfortunate, as it is our duty as citizens to defend and preserve the Constitution, which requires that **we** understand it and not rely upon others to interpret it on our behalf. It is my hope that you, my readers, will become more knowledgeable about the U.S. Constitution, and will gain a more accurate understanding of its purpose and its practical applications in our lives. We the People have been charged with the responsibility to ensure its survival. We must understand its relevance to slow the progress of the United States succumbing to being ruled by a tyrannical and authoritarian government. That said, it is not enough to understand the Constitution. If we are to restore Constitutional principles, we must understand its purpose, teach its underlying philosophy to others, and be vigilant in our efforts to protect it.

Book Conventions

The words we speak influence how we interpret a particular situation; how we *say* it is how we *see* it. Our interpretation of the Constitution is no different. We must realize that the definitions of certain words have changed over the years. Current-day vernacular and word substitutions of its text has altered our interpretation of the Constitution. To better understand the Constitution, we must read and apply its word definitions from the time period in which it was written. Understanding the Framers' intent from over two hundred years ago requires that we apply the word definitions from their era, not ours. It would be unrealistic to expect that we could correctly interpret a document written in 1787 by applying current-day definitions; therefore, I defer to "Noah Webster's 1828 Dictionary of the English Language" as an authoritative source. Webster's 1828 dictionary is considered America's first dictionary. Its definitions span the time period in which the Constitution was written and best captures the meaning of written and spoken words during that era. As an example, compare the written definition of 'marriage' then vs. now:

Marriage (1828 Noah Webster's dictionary) - The act of uniting a man and woman for life; wedlock; the legal union of a man and woman for life. marriage is a contract both civil and religious, by which the parties engage to live together in mutual affection and fidelity, till death shall separate them. marriage was instituted by God himself for the purpose of preventing the promiscuous intercourse of the sexes, for promoting domestic felicity, and for securing the maintenance and education of children.

Marriage (2018 Oxford dictionary) - The legally or formally recognized union of two people as partners in a personal relationship (historically and in some jurisdictions specifically a union between a man and a woman).

Marriage (2018 Merriam-Webster definition) - The state of being united as spouses in a consensual and contractual relationship recognized by law.

The cultural shift since 1828 has redefined the idea of marriage, which necessarily changes its practical application within society. The belief that marriage was instituted by God, as mentioned in Webster's 1828 dictionary, has been removed from recent dictionaries. This example shows how altering the definition of a word, intentionally or not, affects its interpretation and ultimately its application. This premise equally applies to the Constitution. I pose that interpreting the verbiage of the Constitution using modern-day definitions has led us to erroneously conclude that it is a law. For this reason, I have included some relevant definitions throughout this book and within the appendix, using Webster's 1828 dictionary as the source, to support my argument that the Constitution is indeed a contract.

In addition, the word "state" has been purposely capitalized throughout the book for visual emphasis to the importance of individual State independence and sovereignty in relationship to the federal government.

Contracts and The Law

Contracts

When considering the question of why the Constitution is to be regarded as a contract, the best place to start is to review the definition of the word 'contract' and to examine its practical applications:

> Contract - An agreement or covenant between two or more persons, in which each party binds himself to do or forbear some act, and each acquires a right to what the other promises; a mutual promise upon lawful consideration or promise upon lawful consideration or cause, which binds the parties to a performance; a bargain; a compact. Contracts are executory or executed.

As the definition states, a contract formally binds two or more parties together for a mutual benefit and establishes those duties and/or expectations each party promises to carry out. This infers that a contract establishes a binding relationship between the contracting parties. We sometimes give the relationship between the contracting parties a human-friendly name to better identify it; for example, we often call it a partnership, confederation, association, marriage, union, or league.

Contracts are important in that they include specific terms that govern the relationship dynamic between the contracting parties; thus, legal and enforceable contracts must contain certain key elements:

- The contract cannot support illegal activity.
- An offer must be made.
- The parties must promise to act upon or refrain from a particular act.
- Parties to the contract must be competent; they must have the adequate legal and mental capacity to understand the terms and consequences they will be consenting to.
- There must be consideration; something of value must be promised.
- Parties must share an understanding of what the contract represents and what each party is agreeing to. In other words, they must have a "meeting of the minds."
- All parties execute the contract by willfully consenting to its terms. The contract cannot be made under duress.

Most of us are a contracting party to some type of binding relationship or union secured by a contract. Two well-known examples come to mind: marriage and employment. Marriage is the name given to the contractual union formed between spouses, and the spouses secure their union by entering into a religious covenant (contract) and/or civil contract. Their spoken vows represent the terms of their contract, which will govern their union. Each spouse willfully consents to the terms of the union contract by saying "I do" or the like. Similarly, an employment contract establishes a binding relationship between the employer and the employee. The two parties establish a written or implied contract, which lists the expectations and/or restraints of both employer and employee. Both parties then willfully consent to the terms. These two examples - marriage and employment - show how contracts establish a relationship between applicable parties and hold them accountable to perform specific duties and/or maintain certain expectations.

Relationships

As mentioned, contracts are established between two or more parties, creating a legally binding relationship between them. A relationship, in its simplest form, represents a connection or association between people or things. Most of us have some type of established relationship with others: a relationship with a spouse, business associates, neighbors, or members of organizations. As the relationship dynamics are defined by those entering into the contract, no two sets of dynamics are alike: we have different sets of expectations and different ways of fulfilling our obligations. For example, the dynamic between two spouses will be quite different from the dynamic between two business partners. This is to be expected, as the nature of our various relationships dictates expectations specific to that relationship and uniquely established to be beneficial to all involved. There must be some type of mutual understanding between those in the relationship, and there must be certain rules to set expectations and govern the behavior of each participating party. When considered in this context, the Constitution of the United States serves as the political contract that currently binds the current fifty States into a union and establishes certain terms (Articles) written to govern their collective relationship.

10

The Law

It is equally important to speak on the topic of law. A law, in general, exists to regulate something or someone by placing limitations or establishing boundaries. The concept of Law[1] is a broad subject because there are numerous types of laws and their respective meanings and applications are derived from different sources. For example, there is the moral law, common law, statutory law, revealed law, natural law, and the laws of nations - just to name a few. Webster's 1828 dictionary has twenty-six definitions of law. Thus, is it important to specify which type of law is being referenced when speaking to the idea of the Constitution being a law. In current times, Constitutional "Law" seems to be discussed in the context of being similar to statutory[2] law, which are those laws created by a legislative government body for the purpose of regulating the general population. It is my belief that the general population views the Constitution as being the supreme Law that governs "all" within the land (including businesses, organizations, and citizens), with the enforcing powers of statutory law. This would imply that "all" within the land are subject to the Constitution's Articles. I purport that this was **not** the intent of the Framers of the Constitution. On the contrary, the Framers intended for the Constitution to only govern political bodies.

---

1 A law is that which is laid, set or fixed, like statute, constitution, from Latin statuo. A rule, particularly an established or permanent rule, prescribed by the supreme power of a state to its subjects, for regulating their actions, particularly their social actions. Laws are imperative or mandatory, commanding what shall be done; prohibitory, restraining from what is to be forborn; or permissive, declaring what may be done without incurring a penalty.

2 An act of the legislature of a state that extends its binding force to all the citizens or subjects of that state, as distinguished from an act which extends only to an individual or company; an act of the legislature commanding or prohibiting something; a positive law. Statutes are distinguished from common law.

Organic[3] law is another type of law related to the Constitution. Henry Campbell Black's Law Dictionary (1891) defines Organic law as "the fundamental law, or constitution, of a state or nation." Volume One of the United States Code (1926) lists the Constitution of the United States as one of our four Organic laws:

1. The Declaration of Independence
2. The Articles of Confederation
3. Ordinance of 1787: The Northwest Territorial Government
4. Constitution of the United States

This government classification, along with Black's definition, further supports the current belief that the Constitution is actually a law. It should be recognized, however, that Henry Campbell Black's Law dictionary was published over one hundred years after the Constitution was written. Also, the United States Code was not adopted until 1926, which occurred over one hundred thirty-five years after the Constitution was written. These publication dates, established long after the Constitution was written, must be scrutinized when trying to interpret the intended nature of the Constitution. The implication is clear; we should not accept the belief that the Constitution is a law just because Black's Law dictionary and the United States Codes identify it as such. It should be noted that the U.S. Codes also list the Declaration of Independence as one of the four Organic Laws, which is obviously not the case in the current meaning and application of the word. The purpose of a declaration is to proclaim something, not regulate behavior. The Declaration of Independence's purpose, as

3 The fundamental law, or constitution, of a state or nation, written or unwritten; that law or system of laws or principles which defines and establishes the organization of its government.

professed in its name, was to declare independence, not to establish law. The fifty-six signers of the Declaration of Independence were advocates for independence from the British crown and motherland. Their signatures did not establish statutory law, as that was not their intent, nor did they have the authority to do so. The U.S. Constitution and Declaration of Independence are listed as two of our four Organic laws, but neither are statutory in nature.

Contract & Law

Contracts and laws serve distinct purposes. A contract formally binds parties together for mutual agreement, whereas a law establishes specific rules of conduct and regulates certain actions and behaviors of the those who are a party to the contract. Regarding civil government laws, only those with legislative authority can enact statutory law, while anyone who meets basic legal requirements can enter into a contract. In the context of the Constitution, it cannot be mostly a law *and* a contract; it has to primarily be one or the other. The functionary differences between a contract and law can be applied to help make that determination:

Contract	Law, bylaw, rule, regulation
Binds two or more parties together to do or forbear some act	Regulates the behavior or actions of something, or the intercourse between things
Can be created by any person/organization that meets certain contract requirements	Can only be established by those parties with the authority to do so
Can only be altered/dissolved by the contracting parties	Can only be altered/repealed by those parties with the authority to do so

Contract (*continued*)	Law, bylaw, rule, regulation
Established to provide mutual benefits to the contracting parties	Allows for punitive consequences for violating the law, bylaw, rule, term, or regulation

I purport that the Constitution is primarily a contract whose initial purpose was to bind the several States together into a new federated union. Secondly, the contract's underlying seven Articles were drafted to establish a federal government (i.e., the Government of the United States), delegate this new governing body specific and limited powers, and to regulate the intercourse between the several States of the Union. It must be noted that the relational order between a contract and law is significant in that a contract must precede a law. This means that a binding contract must be established between the contracting parties before the parties are subjected to the contract's underlying terms or rules. This order applies to statutory law as well, in that those who will be governed by statutory law must first willfully consent to be governed. In other words, there must be an established contract between the government and the governed before any laws are imposed upon the general population. Attempting to impose a law upon the governed (i.e., We the People) without our prior consent is a government violation of our individual inalienable rights to autonomy, self-authority, and personal liberty. This is a fundamental premise stated within the Declaration of Independence:

> We hold these truths to be self-evident, that all men are created equal, that they are endowed by their Creator with certain unalienable Rights, that among these are Life, Liberty and the pursuit of Happiness.-- That to secure these

rights, Governments are instituted among Men, deriving their just powers from the consent of the governed.

The Declaration of Independence mentions that governments are established to secure (protect) our inalienable rights, and the government's just[4] powers are derived from the consent of the governed (i.e., We, the People). If we are to say that the Constitution is [statutory] law, then we should be able to identify which founding document serves as the active contract that precedes and undergirds the Constitution. However, that would impossible as no such contract exists. This is because the Constitution of the United States *is* the current contract.

Homeowners' Association

A homeowners' association [HOA] is a current-day relationship that closely aligns with the underlying political structure of the United States and supports the argument that the Constitution is a political contract. This is based on the concept of associations:

> Association - The act of associating; union; connection of persons. Union of persons in a company; a society formed for transacting or carrying on some business for mutual advantage; a partnership. It is often applied to a union of states or a confederacy.

An association is a type of relationship; thus, a homeowners' association represents the intangible relationship established among the various homeowners within a community for their mutual benefit. As supported by the above definition, discrete entities

---

4 (upright/honest)

normally enter into such a relationship for mutual advantage; and the association "is often applied to a union of States or a confederacy." When reflecting upon the purpose and structure of the Articles of Confederation (1777), this concept of an association immediately comes to mind. Similar to a homeowners' association, the original thirteen States entered into a political contract under the Articles of Confederation to form a perpetual union (i.e., a connection) among themselves for mutual benefit:

> Articles of Confederation (Article III)
>
> The said states hereby severally enter into a firm league of friendship with each other, for their common defence, the security of their Liberties, and their mutual and general welfare, binding themselves to assist each other, against all force offered to, or attacks made upon them, or any of them, on account of religion, sovereignty, trade, or any other pretence whatever.

A homeowners' association (HOA) is a good example to reference because the relationship between the homeowners is similar to that of the States that make up the United States. Whereas the homeowners' relationship is similar to that of the States under the Articles of Confederation, the HOA governing body that governs the homeowners' association is similar to the "Government of the United States" (i.e., federal government) formed by the States under the U.S. Constitution:

Imagine a neighborhood that contains thirteen homes. The collective homeowners decide to enter into a contract for mutual benefits. Each homeowner, being sovereign and independent from the others, governs the affairs of his/her home as they see fit. Each of the thirteen homeowners can do whatever they want, whenever they want, in any way they like. This being the case, now imagine a scenario where a couple of the homeowners have painted their homes with colors that create an eyesore; three of the homeowners consistently fail to maintain their home and surrounding areas; and internal conflicts repeatedly arise among several homeowners within the community. When situations such as these occur, the individual homeowners gradually come to realize that their freedoms and autonomy—as great as they appear—are creating challenges within the collective neighborhood. These issues are creating a financial decline in neighborhood property value and causing an increase in arguments among the homeowners. Although the issues are obvious, but without a mutual agreement in place, the homeowners feel powerless to do anything about it because they acknowledge and respect each homeowner's independence and sovereignty. Who then, if anyone, should regulate the relationship and adjudicate over such conflicts? The homeowners who are inclined to speak up find themselves in conflict with others who disagree; thus, nothing is addressed or resolved. When they, as a group, recognize that absolute sovereignty is not working out for the neighborhood, they realize that something must be done. After several discussions, the collective homeowners conclude that all would benefit if they were to formally establish an association among themselves for mutual benefits. For example, the homeowners could help protect each other's property; they could combine a portion of their monies to build community additions, such as a playground for the kids; they could share their collective knowledge to improve their individual and collective situations. The homeowners also conclude that their new association (i.e., relationship) should be supported by a binding contract. The contract would explicitly list those articles (terms) that govern their newly established relationship by setting expectations and restraints. After the homeowners consent to establishing a formal relationship and a binding contract, they name their new union the "Homeowners' Association" (i.e., the association among homeowners). Although they have established a contract among them, they realize that no provisions have been made to enforce its terms. Something else is needed. The homeowners later decide to establish an external governing body to govern their association (relationship). It is decided that the new governing body will *serve* the homeowners by:

- establishing certain rules that will better support the relationship among the homeowners (legislative branch).
- ensuring the homeowners are adhering to the terms of their contract (executive branch).
- impartially adjudicate over conflicts that may arise between the homeowners (judicial branch).

The homeowners name the governing body the "Homeowners' Association Governing Board." Considering that the external governing body is not a member of the actual homeowners' association, nor a party to the homeowners' binding contract, the homeowners decide that it would be best if the Homeowners' Association Governing Board's powers be limited, in order to prohibit government overreach. The homeowners amend their HOA contract to include this clause.

Now, imagine that these thirteen homes represented the original thirteen States that made up the United States of America. Like the homeowners, the individual States came to realize the benefits and dangers of absolute independence and sovereignty; thus, the States *united* to establish a confederation (i.e., relationship) for mutual benefits. Whereas the homeowners named the association established among them the "Homeowners' Association," the States named the confederation among them the "United States." Like the homeowners, the States entered into a [political] contract among themselves (i.e., the Articles of Confederation). The contract's underlying thirteen articles would govern their relationship. The States later replaced the Articles of Confederation with a new political contract (i.e., the Constitution of the United States). The new contract established an external governing body called the "Government of the United States" (b.k.a. the federal government) whose primary duties were to:

- establish laws that would govern the union (relationship) among the States (legislative branch).
- enforce the terms of the States' contract and future union laws (executive branch).
- adjudicate over conflicts that may arise between the States (judicial branch).

If should be emphasized that the HOA governing board and the Federal government are ***external*** governing bodies. Just as the HOA governing board is not a member of the Homeowners' Association, the Federal government is not a member of the United States. As such, the responsibility of the HOA governing board is restricted to governing the ***relationship*** among the homeowners. Similarly, the responsibility of the Federal government is ***restricted to the governance of the relationship that exists among the States and does not extend to governing the States themselves.*** The HOA board and the federal government are similar in their makeup and duties:

Homeowners' Association	Federal Government
The HOA covenant represents the contract that exists between the homeowners	The U.S. Constitution represents the contract that exists among the States in the union
Each homeowner governs the internal affairs of their own home	Each State governs its own internal affairs
The HOA governing board is comprised of those individuals that own a home within the neighborhood	The federal governing body is comprised of citizens of the United States
The homeowners have a right to protect their homes from threats	The various member States have the right to protect their State from threats
The HOA governing board has the duty of protecting the community as a whole	The federal government has the duty of protecting the Union as a whole
The homeowners pay dues to the HOA governing body to financially support its delegated duties	The States pay taxes to the federal government to financially supports its delegated duties

The States

The Colonies Declare Themselves as States

This section provides some historical background to establish the framework of how the States became a union and how the U.S. Constitution eventually became their current-day contract. Below I have listed the key events which took place:

- The original thirteen colonies declared themselves "Free and Independent States"; declared their right to self-governance; absolved themselves of their allegiance to the British Crown; and severed all political ties between themselves and their motherland: Great Britain.
- The newly established thirteen States formally entered into a perpetual union under the Articles of Confederation.
- The "Articles of Confederation" were replaced by the Constitution of the United States.

These events, coupled with a basic understanding of contracts, laws, relationships, and unions will support the assertion that the U.S. Constitution is a contract and not a law.

Separation from Great Britain

The original thirteen States that made up the United States were previously British colonies.[1] The thirteen colonies resided on the Northern American continent and operated under the authority of the King's charter,[2] who, himself, resided in the far-distant motherland of Great Britain. Over time, the physical distance that separated the colonies from their motherland created problems that warranted action. This became apparent during the mid- to late eighteenth century. During that era, the colonies that operated under the charter of King George III had local needs, concerns, and challenges. The problem was that when these issues arose, their far-distant king could not readily address them, refused to address them, or chose to address them in a tyrannical manner. The abuses suffered under King George III became so odious that the thirteen colonies formally declared their independence and absolved themselves from the British Crown, thereby proclaiming that they ought to be free and independent States:

Lee Resolution (1776)

Resolved, That these United Colonies are, and of right ought to be, free and independent States, that they are absolved from

---

1 A company or body of people transplanted from their mother country to a remote province or country to cultivate and inhabit it, and remaining subject to the jurisdiction of the parent state; as the British colonies in America or the Indies; the Spanish colonies in South America. When such settlements cease to be subject to the parent state, they are no longer denominated colonies.

2 In its more usual sense, it is the instrument of a grant conferring powers, rights and privileges, either from a king or other sovereign power, or from a private person, as a charter of exemption, that no person shall be empannelled on a jury, a charter of pardon, etc. The charters under which most of the colonies in America were settled, were given by the king of England, and incorporated certain persons, with powers to hold the lands granted, to establish a government, and make laws for their own regulation. These were called charter-governments.

all allegiance to the British Crown, and that all political connection between them and the State of Great Britain is, and
ought to be, totally dissolved.

That it is expedient forthwith to take the most effectual measures for forming foreign Alliances.

That a plan of confederation be prepared and transmitted to the
respective Colonies for their consideration and approbation.

The Lee Resolution (1776) was followed by the Declaration of
Independence (1776). The Declaration of Independence is an
important document, in that it challenged and redefined the hierarchal position and role of government. It put forth the self-evident
truth that all men[3] are created equal, with inalienable rights; and
that governments are established to secure (protect) such rights.
The Declaration reinforced the idea that the Colonies ought to
have the right to be Free and Independent States and are absolved
from all allegiance to the British Crown. The Declaration of
Independence listed certain abuses that the Colonies suffered
under King George III, which further justified their right to
declare independence. Committed to their common goal of achiev-
ing independence, those who signed the Declaration, along with
those who supported it, established a pact in which they pledged
their lives, their fortunes, and their sacred honor to each other:

Declaration of Independence (1776)
We, therefore, the Representatives of the united [sic] States of
America, in General Congress, Assembled, appealing to the
Supreme Judge of the world for the rectitude of our intentions,

---

3 18th century vernacular of mankind. The race or species of human beings.

do, in the Name, and by Authority of the good People of these Colonies, solemnly publish and declare, That these United Colonies are, and of Right ought to be Free and Independent States; that they are Absolved from all Allegiance to the British Crown, and that all political connection between them and the State of Great Britain, is and ought to be totally dissolved; and that as Free and Independent States, they have full Power to levy War, conclude Peace, contract Alliances, establish Commerce, and to do all other Acts and Things which Independent States may of right do.

Each of the thirteen States, declaring themselves to be "Free and Independent States" in the Declaration, proceeded to set up their respective State governments, laws, and constitutions—independent of the other States.

The States

> State - A political body, or body politic; the whole body of people united under one government, whatever may be the form of the government.

Before speaking further on the collective relationship among the States, it is important to understand what the Founders and Framers meant when referencing a State. A State is a body politic,[4] which represents the entire body of people united under their own system of government; thus, when the Framers spoke of a State, it was a political rather than a geographical reference. For example, the State

---

4 The whole body of people united under one government.

of Georgia is representative of the whole body of people united under one government; the State of Nebraska is its own government body politic, separate and independent from the government and body politic that makes up the State of Texas, and so on. In the context of being a political body, each State is identified by those collective persons living within its territorial borders. The territorial borders separate each State and its government from those of other States. Each of the fifty States was founded upon the understanding that it could operate politically independently of the other States in the Union. At the same time, each State agreed to unite with the others for mutual benefit. Per the Declaration of Independence, the States declared themselves free and independent of the British Crown while establishing that they were also independent of each other. This structure is still in effect. Each State, then and now, has its own constitution, legislative branch, executive branch, supreme Court, laws, flag, and president (i.e., governor[5]). As such, each State, being sovereign and independent of the others, was free to govern itself as it saw fit, which is technically still the case. It is important to note that the States have never forfeited their independence nor sovereignty, as initially proclaimed in the Declaration of Independence, the Treaty of Paris, the Articles of Confederation, and the U.S. Constitution. Forfeiture of one's independence or autonomy is not required as a condition of entering into a union, association, confederation, federation, or a league. The several States are no different; each retains their independence and sovereignty as a condition of joining the union. Although the later results of the Civil War (a.k.a. the War between the States) invalidated the

---

5 One who is invested with supreme authority to administer or enforce the laws; the supreme executive magistrate of a state, community, corporation or post. Thus, in America, each state has its governor; Canada has its governor.

Confederate States' natural right to independence, some State constitutions still lay claim to independence and self-governance:

Texas State constitution (Article I. Bill of Rights)

That the general, great and essential principles of liberty and free government may be recognized and established, we declare: Sec. 1. FREEDOM AND SOVEREIGNTY OF STATE. Texas is a free and independent State, subject only to the Constitution of the United States, and the maintenance of our free institutions and the perpetuity of the Union depend upon the preservation of the right of local self-government, unimpaired to all the States.

Massachusetts State constitution (Article IV)

The people of this commonwealth have the sole and exclusive right of governing themselves, as a free, sovereign, and independent state; and do, and forever hereafter shall, exercise and enjoy every power, jurisdiction, and right, which is not, or may not hereafter, be by them expressly delegated to the United States of America in Congress assembled.

New Hampshire State constitution (Article VII)

The people of this state have the sole and exclusive right of governing themselves as a free, sovereign, and independent state; and do, and forever hereafter shall, exercise and enjoy every power, jurisdiction, and right, pertaining thereto, which is not, or may not hereafter be, by them expressly delegated to the United States of America in congress assembled.

Identifying a State as being a political body makes it easier to comprehend that the "United States" is a union among fifty "united" political bodies. Unfortunately, the current day belief that the United States is a single country clouds our political understanding and prevents us from seeing the proper relationship between the various States and their collective relationship with the federal government. Thus, the idea and importance of State independence has waned, often due to political ignorance, individual apathy, and by the States' authority being usurped by the federal government - an entity which is categorically not part of the United States.

Founding Organic Documents

The Articles of Confederation (1777)

> Confederate - United in a league; allied by treaty; engaged in a confederacy. To unite in a league; to join in a mutual contract or covenant. The colonies of America confederated in 1775. Several States of Europe have sometimes confederated for mutual safety.

The Declaration of Independence declared that each of the thirteen States ought to be free and independent; however, expressing something does not automatically make it so. Some type of action must still be taken to turn a declaration into reality. The fifty-six men who signed the Declaration, and all those who supported State liberation from their motherland, understood that they would likely have to engage in war with Great Britain to attain independence. King George III, the British king at that time, was not going to simply concede to the States' desire to separate from the British Crown. Those fighting for their independence knew it was going to be a difficult feat, considering that Great Britain had the best navy in the world at the time. To make matters worse, the States would also have to protect themselves from other possible foreign invasions, considering they no longer benefited from their motherland's protection—the same motherland with which they were about to engage in war. Seeing the challenges that lay ahead, the States understood that if they were to unite, their chances of succeeding in defending themselves and defeating Great Britain's impending military offensive would be greatly increased; thus, the thirteen States formally established a confederation (union) by entering into a political contract: The Articles of Confederation (1777). As previously mentioned, unions of all types (i.e., associations, confederations, leagues, etc.) require a written or implied contract/compact or agreement that formally binds their members together for the mutual benefit of a common cause or belief. The Articles of Confederation served as the States' political contract, which would bind them together into a confederation[1] and govern their relationship. The union contract contained thirteen Articles[2] that listed the terms to which every State would agree to adhere as a condition of joining the confederation. The Articles of Confederation's preamble acknowledged that the thirteen States, confirmed by their respective delegates, agreed to the specific articles (terms) of the contract and mutually agreed to form a perpetual union:

Articles of Confederation (preamble)

To all to whom these Presents shall come, we, the undersigned Delegates of the States affixed to our Names send greeting. Whereas the Delegates of the United States of America in Con-

1 The act of confederating; a league; a compact for mutual support; alliance; particularly of princes, nations or states. The United States of America are sometimes called the confederation

2 A single clause in a contract, account system of regulations, treaty, or other writing; a particular separate charge or item, in an account; a term, condition, or stipulation, in a contract.

gress assembled did on the fifteenth day of November in the year of our Lord One Thousand Seven Hundred and Seventy seven, and in the Second Year of the Independence of America agree to certain articles of Confederation and perpetual Union between the States of Newhampshire, Massachusetts-bay, Rhodeisland [Rhode Island] and Providence Plantations, Connecticut, New York, New Jersey, Pennsylvania, Delaware, Maryland, Virginia, North Carolina, South Carolina, and Georgia in the Words following, viz. "Articles of Confederation and perpetual Union between the States of Newhampshire [New Hampshire], Massachusetts-bay, Rhodeisland and Providence Plantations, Connecticut, New York, New Jersey, Pennsylvania, Delaware, Maryland, Virginia, North Carolina, South Carolina, and Georgia.

A name was given to the newly formed confederation between the thirteen States; Article I of the Union contract mentions that the name of the confederacy was to be called "The United States of America":

Articles of Confederation (Article I)
The Stile [style] of this confederacy shall be, "The United States of America."

Article II mentions that each State retains its sovereignty, freedom, and independence. This supports the premise that entering into a union does not forfeit the participant's sovereignty, freedom, or independence (my emphasis):

Articles of Confederation (Article II)

Each state retains its sovereignty, freedom, and independence, and every power, jurisdiction, and right, which is not by this Confederation expressly delegated to the United States, in Congress assembled.

Article III provides some reasons why the States formed the union (i.e., for mutual benefits):

Articles of Confederation (Article III)

The said states hereby severally enter into a firm league of friendship with each other, for their common defence [defense], the security of their Liberties, and their mutual and general welfare, binding themselves to assist each other, against all force offered to, or attacks made upon them, or any of them, on account of religion, sovereignty, trade, or any other pretence whatever.

The States ratified the adoption of the Articles of Confederation at different times, officially activating their first political contract as the United States:

1. Virginia   December 16, 1777

2. South Carolina   February 5, 1778

3. New York   February 6, 1778

4. Rhode Island   February 9, 1778

5. Connecticut   February 12, 1778

6. Georgia   February 26, 1778

7. New Hampshire   March 4, 1778

8. Pennsylvania	March 5, 1778
9. Massachusetts	March 10, 1778
10. North Carolina	April 5, 1778
11. New Jersey	November 19, 1778
12. Delaware	February 1, 1779
13. Maryland	February 2, 1781

1783 Treaty of Paris

As history has shown, the States eventually won their independence from Great Britain as a result of the American Revolutionary War (a.k.a. the War of Independence). A peace treaty was signed in Paris, France (September 3rd, 1783) to signify the end of the war. Article I of the treaty required that the British King acknowledge each State as being sovereign and independent:

1783 Treaty of Paris (The Definitive Treaty of Peace 1783)

Article 1st

His Brittanic Majesty acknowledges the said United States, viz., New Hampshire, Massachusetts Bay, Rhode Island and Providence Plantations, Connecticut, New York, New Jersey, Pennsylvania, Delaware, Maryland, Virginia, North Carolina, South Carolina and Georgia, to be free sovereign and Independent States; that he treats with them as such, and for himself his Heirs & Successors, relinquishes all claims to the Government, Propriety, and Territorial Rights of the same and every Part thereof.

Each State was listed separately to emphasize their independence from the British Crown **and** from the other States in the union. Each State had the right (just claim) to govern its affairs independently from the other States. Each established its own governing body, constitution, laws, and flag of symbolic distinction - all of which remain in effect today.

Country or Union?

Turn to any media source and you will find that the United States is frequently referenced as being a country. This reference has become part of our general political speak and conversations. We have been educated to believe that the United States is a country. To further reinforce this current perspective, the 48 continental[1] States share common borders with each other, which give the visual appearance that the collective States are **one** country. Unfortunately, the "United States" and "Country" have become synonymous terms which, I suspect, is the major reason why so many Americans have an incorrect understanding of the United States, the U.S. Constitution, and our unique system of government. Referencing the "United States" as a country reinforces our belief that we are one collective entity (singular) rather than as multiple independent entities (plural). This notion brings us back to our duly apt adage: that what we call ourselves is how we see ourselves. To challenge current conventional beliefs, it should be noted that our organic founding documents[2] never reference the United States as being a country,

[1] In America, pertaining to the United States, as continental money, in distinction from what pertains to the separate states; a word much used during the revolution.

[2] Declaration of Independence, Articles of Confederation, Constitution of the United States, and Northwest Ordinance

and for good reason: because the United States is **not** a country; it is a union (relationship) between political bodies. The current union is comprised of fifty separate and independent States, not fifty States merged into one country; thus, the "United States" should be interpreted as a political term, not a geographical one. Referencing the United States as a union going forward, rather than a country, is important because there are important distinctions between the two:

Country	Union
Singular entity	Multiple entities (i.e., fifty States)
A geographical tract of land; territory	A relationship among entities
Geographical location	General, non-specific location
Tangible land	Intangible relationship

Country

Because a country and a union are not synonymous in their nature, the "United States" cannot be both a country and a union. The organic founding documents make it clear that the United States was established as a union, so our current-day reference to it being a country is incorrect. It is important to note, however, that some of the delegates referenced "country" several times during the Constitutional Convention held in Philadelphia. George Washington, the first president of the new federation and the chosen president of the Philadelphia Constitutional Convention, referenced "Country" five times in his first presidential inaugural speech. Surely, **he** would have known that the United States is a union! Likewise, Alexander Hamilton mentioned "country" in his opening introduction of the Federalist Papers. He, too, would have known that the United States is a union. Just as we do today, many others during that time referenced "country" or "countrymen" in their general and political conversations; however, the reference must be framed in its proper context. The Framers and Founders understood that the word "country" represented a physical tract of land or territory;[3] a geographical location; the tract of land or territory where they and others **physically** resided. On the other hand, when they referenced the United States, they were specifically speaking of the political relationship that existed among the member states of the Union. In current times, we speak of the United States of America as being a country rather than a political union. Doing so paints the picture that the U.S. Constitution is a "Law" that governs a whole country rather than a contract that governs the relationship that exists among political bodies.

Union

A union[4] joins two or more entities together. These entities can consist of people, organizations, businesses, States, countries, etc. Regarding the fifty States that comprise the United States, the Webster's 1828 Dictionary definition of union denotes "states united."

---

3 The extent or compass of land within the bounds or belonging to the jurisdiction of any state, city or other body. A tract of land belonging to and under the dominion of a prince or state, lying at a distance from the parent country or from the seat of government; as the territories of the East India Company; the territories of the United States; the territory of Michigan; Northwest territory These districts of country, when received into the union and acknowledged to be states, lose the appellation of territory

4 The act of joining two or more things into one, and thus forming a compound body or a mixture; or the junction or coalition of things thus united. union differs from connection, as it implies the bodies to be in contact, without an intervening body; whereas things may be connected by the intervention of a third body, as by a cord or chain. States united. Thus the United States of America are sometimes call the union

Union (1828 Noah Webster's dictionary) - States united. Thus the United States of America are sometimes call the union.

Unions are known by different names. They are sometimes called associations, leagues, confederations, and federations. The specific term used to reference the union helps us to identify the type of relationship and the dynamic among the various entities:

- Marriage: the term given to the union between spouses
- Partnership: the term often given to the union between business entities
- Homeowners' Association (HOA): the term given to the union between homeowners
- Teacher's Union: the term given to the union between teachers
- National Football League: the term given to the union between several football teams
- European Union: the term given to the union established between certain European countries
- United States: the name given to the union of the several States

The above examples all require some form of contract or agreement to bind its members together and govern the mutual intercourse that exists between them. For example, businesses that unite for a mutual benefit require a contract between them; organizations that unite require a binding agreement; the football teams that make up the National Football **League** (NFL) have a binding contract between them as well. Speaking of, the NFL is a popular modern-day example whose league closely resembles the framework and relationship of the various States that make up the United States:

The National Football League	The United States
Thirty-two independent teams	Fifty independent States
Each NFL team operates independently of the others	Each State operates independently of the others
The member teams have a binding contract: Constitution and Bylaws of the NFL (Est. Feb 1, 1970)	The member States have a binding contract: Constitution of the United States (Est. Sept 17, 1787)
The contract contains articles that govern the intercourse among the member teams	The contract contains articles that govern the intercourse between the member States
The contract establishes an external governing body (i.e., League Commissioner)	The contract establishes an external governing body (i.e., the Government of the United States)
Name of the relationship: National Football League	Name of the relationship: United States
Union type = league	Union type = federation

These are a few examples that show the similarities between the NFL and the USA. Examining the respective contracts between the NFL teams and the States will reveal additional ones. For example, Article II of the NFL's constitution lists the "Purpose and Objects" (i.e., mutual benefits) of the union. Likewise, the Constitution's preamble and Article III of the Articles of Confederation lists the mutual benefits for establishing the union between the States.

Unity Does Not Forfeit Sovereignty

It is important to stress that the States did not forfeit their sovereignty by joining the United States. The several States formed a federation union, established a political contract between themselves, created Articles that would govern their relationship, and created an external governing body (i.e., the federal government) that would *serve* the States by governing their political relationship; not govern over the States themselves. The several States joined the union for mutual benefits. That being said, it is important to emphasize that the purpose of associations, leagues, confederations, and unions is to improve the condition or position of its members; therefore, joining an association or a union should provide benefits to its members, not rob them of their individuality, independence, or sovereignty, etc. If forfeiting one's identity, independence, or sovereignty is the consequence of joining a union, then the purpose and benefits of joining are defeated.

> Ex #1: Marriage, being a union, is supposed to provide mutual benefits and strengthen the positions of both spouses. The spouses unite with the expectation of receiving benefits that come with doing so. A certain amount of concession is expected, but it should not be to the degree where the spouses lose their independence or individuality. Each spouse should retain their autonomy and individuality, which includes ownership of their thoughts, ideas, likes, dislikes, feelings, and ambitions. This is the underlying premise of all unions, leagues, and associations, regardless of type.

> Ex #2: The countries that currently make up the European "Union" (my emphasis) preserve their sovereign independence as a condition of joining the union. This same premise of unification applies to the current fifty

states that make up the "United States." Each State joined the union for mutual gain, not for individual loss. The original thirteen States were adamant about retaining the independence and sovereignty that they had fought so hard to attain, and these beliefs were reiterated in their political writings. The States understood that unity does not negate or forfeit sovereignty and independence.

America is a Continent, not a Country

Now that it has been shown that the "United States" is not a country, it is equally important to address another misnomer - making "America"[5] synonymous with "country." Like the United States, "America" is often referenced as being a country, which is not the case. America is the given name of a continent. This being the case, a country and continent cannot be synonymous terms. Conflating the two terms adds yet another layer of confusion to understanding the system and function of government established by the Framers of the Constitution. For example, conflating the United States and America to both mean "country" would translate the "United States of America" to mean "Country of Country." An accurate translation of the "United States of America" requires that we examine the relationship between the three components that make up the name:

---

5 One of the great continents, first discovered by Sebastian Cabot, June 11, O.S. 1498, and by Columbus, or Christoval Colon, Aug. 1, the same year. It extends from the eightieth degree of North, to the fifty-fourth degree of South Latitude; and from the thirty-fifth to the one hundred and fifty-sixth degree of Longitude West from Greenwich, being about nine thousand miles in length. Its breadth at Darien is narrowed to about forty-five miles, but at the northern extremity is nearly four thousand miles. From Darien to the North, the continent is called North america and to the South, it is called South america

United States - the name of the union among the States (i.e., States united).

Of - a preposition that describes the relationship between two things. In this case, "Of" connects "United States" with "America."

America - the combined landmass that makes up the North and South American continents.

Thus, an accurate translation of the "United States of America" would be: The Union between political bodies (States) that physically reside on the continent of [North] America. This premise also applied to the "Confederate States of America", the name of the union established between the Southern States that seceded from the United States. The Northern States named their union the United States; the Southern States named their union the Confederate States. As previously mentioned, a union and a confederation represent a relationship between things. In this case, they represent a relationship between the various States.

The European Union

The European Union is another comparative example to the United States, in that the European union is comprised of several European countries that united for mutual benefits. The various European countries named their political relationship the "European Union." The European Union, like other unions - including the United States - established a contract that formally bound the member countries together. Their contract (i.e., Constitution of the European Union) contains underlying Articles established to govern the intercourse among the member countries. Similar to the fifty member states of the United States, each member country of the European Union is sovereign and independent of the others, which is symbolized by their respective flags. France, for example, cannot dictate the affairs of Germany, nor vice versa. Similarly, in the United States the state of Texas (being an independent body politic) cannot dictate the affairs of Maine, nor vice versa. The European Union and the United States are similar in many ways:

European Union	United States (Union)
Comprised of several independent countries	Comprised of several independent political bodies called "States"
Each member country has its own government and laws, independent of the other countries in the Union	Each member State has its own government and laws, independent of the other States in the Union
Each member country has its own flag, which is symbolic of its identity and sovereignty	Each Member State has its own flag, which is symbolic of its identity and sovereignty
There is one union flag that represents the European Union as a whole	There is one union flag that represents the United States as a whole
A political contract (constitution) exists between the member countries of the Union	A political contract (constitution) exists between the member States of the Union
Each member country has its own constitution independent of the Union's constitution	Each Member State has its own constitution independent of the Union's constitution
Each member country willfully joined the Union	Each member State willfully joined the Union

A More Perfect Union

Written as a political contract, the Articles of Confederation established a perpetual union between the original thirteen States. The contract presented thirteen articles outlining the terms that would govern the union between the member States. The intent was for the member States to agree to adhere to the terms. However, like any contract, this was not always the case. Contracts are sometimes breached. Furthermore, the Articles of Confederation lacked a governing body with sufficient authority to enforce its terms. Lack of adherence and enforcement rendered the contract impractical, thus weakening the overall strength and integrity of the union. It soon became clear that it was important to address this issue and other inherent flaws. For this reason, the States staged a convention[6] in Philadelphia, PA (1787). The purpose was to address flaws within the Articles of Confederation and other matters related to the union. Except for Rhode Island, each of the twelve States sent delegates[7] to Philadelphia to represent their State's interest in the union. It was at this convention that the Constitution of the United States was drafted.

It is important to note that the delegates in attendance acted as representatives of their respective States. They were not delegated legislative powers. That is to say, they did **not** have the necessary powers to create any statutory laws that would govern the States or their respective citizens. As this is the case, we must conclude that the Constitution was never conceived as statutory law, as is

---

6 An assembly. In this sense, the word includes any formal meeting or collection of men for civil or ecclesiastical purposes; particularly an assembly of delegates or representatives for consultation on important concerns, civil, political or ecclesiastical. In the United States, this name is given to the assembly of representatives which forms a constitution of government, or political association; as the convention which formed the constitution of the United States in 1787.

7 A person appointed and sent by another with powers to transact business as his representative; a deputy; a commissioner; a vicar. In the United States, a person elected or appointed to represent a state or a district, in the Congress, or in a Convention for forming or altering a constitution.

so often implied in political discussions. This also means that the reference to "Law" within Article VI of the Constitution must be reexamined for its proper context and application. Lastly, if we *are* to believe that the Constitution is statutory law, then we *must* also conclude that the delegates engaged in an unjust act of conversion, by converting their powers from that of delegator to lawmaker.

After much debate, the delegates proposed to dissolve the confederation union that existed between the States and replace it with a new federated union. This also meant that the existing contract between the States (i.e., The Articles of Confederation) would be replaced by a new one (i.e., The Constitution of the United States). The new contract would also establish an external governing body (i.e., The Government of the United States). Similar to the Articles of Confederation, the Constitution's preamble mentions the mutual benefits of the new union:

> Constitution of the United States (Preamble)
> We the People of the United States, in Order to form a more perfect Union, establish Justice, insure domestic Tranquility, provide for the common defence [defense], promote the general Welfare, and secure the Blessings of Liberty to ourselves and our Posterity, do ordain and establish this Constitution for the United States of America.

What is a Constitution?

The Constitution of the United States and the fifty State constitutions are important political documents that have existed for decades. The U.S. Constitution, especially, is the topic of countless political conversations. Political junkies and political parties on both sides often reference and quote the U.S. Constitution to debate and support their political ideology. The State constitutions are occasionally mentioned, but I have found that many Americans are unaware of their existence, as emphasis on the U.S. Constitution has taken precedence. As much as we hear and talk about the various constitutions, their purpose is rarely discussed or explained. The current consensus seems to purport that constitutions are [statutory] laws meant to govern the country and/or state, including both the private and public sectors of society. I purport that this is not the case. Contrary to popular belief, the purpose of the various constitutions[1] found throughout the United States is to establish a government and delegate to it specific duties and powers to support the government's duty of securing the inalienable rights of individuals. This established

---

1 The established form of government in a state, kingdom or country; a system of fundamental rules, principles and ordinances for the government of a state or nation. In free states, the constitution is paramount to the statutes or laws enacted by the legislature, limiting and controlling its power; and in the United States, the legislature is created, and its powers designated, by the constitution

government duty is the undergird for every State constitution and a founding principle within the Declaration of Independence:

> "We hold these truths to be self-evident, that all men are created equal, that they are endowed by their Creator with certain unalienable Rights, that among these are Life, Liberty and the pursuit of Happiness. - That to secure these rights, Governments are instituted among Men, deriving their just powers from the consent of the governed..."

Because civil government is an authoritative institution that implement its policies using force and coercion, constitutions are especially important in that they attempt to limit the government's powers by explicitly stating what the government **can** do rather than what it **cannot**. A State constitution, which represent the political contract between the State and its citizens, delegates specific and limited powers to the State governments as a way to limit its force and authority upon its citizens. Similarly, the Constitution of the United States, which represents the political contract among the States, established the Government of the United States[2] (i.e., the federal government) and delegated to it specific duties and enumerated[3] powers to limit its authority upon the union. Because a constitution represents a political document used for establishing a governing body, its verbiage is directed only towards government and political institutions, not entities within the private sector. That is to say, constitutions do **not** delegate powers or rights to private-sector individuals or businesses, since these entities are not political in nature.

---

2 Currently referred to as the Federal Government
3 The act of counting or telling a number, by naming each particular.

Modern Relevancy of the Constitution

As of the writing of this book, the Constitution of the United States is approaching 233 years of existence. Many people believe that the Constitution is outdated, and its original purpose and underlying laws are irrelevant for current times. Some believe that the Constitution should be rewritten for modern relevancy. This line of thinking is probably rooted in the current belief that the Constitution is a law. If that were true, it is conceivable that it might be antiquated and therefore inadequate for addressing current-day challenges. However, if we view it as a binding union contract that exists among the States, it remains entirely relevant. That is to say, the States cannot technically remain "united" (i.e., United States) if they lack a common agreement among them that governs their union. The Constitution's underlying Articles exist to govern the union by establishing terms to which the political bodies are expected to adhere. The Constitution also remains relevant in that it helps to protect our inalienable rights and liberties by placing limits on governmental authority, as history has proven several times that a government without limitations on its authority and without proper "checks and balances" will eventually become tyrannical. The Constitution also helps hedge against government tyranny by distributing powers between the States and the federal government, and across three branches (legislative, executive, judicial) at the local, State, and federal levels. For the above-mentioned reasons alone, the U.S. Constitution remains as relevant today as it was in 1787.

State Constitutions

Each of the fifty States governments, being independent political bodies, is a party to two different political contracts.

The first contract is the State's own constitution, which represents the political contract between the State and its citizens. The citizens of each State delegate specific duties and powers to their State government via their State constitution. The State government, in turn, uses its constitutionally delegated powers to govern the interrelationship that exists between its citizens. The second contract is the Constitution of the United States, which is the political contract that exists between the member States of the Union. Its underlying Articles delegate certain powers to the federal government and also govern the interrelationships that exist between the States. It is important to note that the federal government is not a State, nor does it reside within a State; thus, it does not have a State constitution, nor is it a member of the United States.

The U.S. Constitution is a Contract

> Compact - An agreement; a contract between parties; a word that may be applied, in a general sense, to any covenant or contract between individuals; but it is more generally applied to agreements between nations and states, as treaties and confederacies. *The constitution of the United States, therefore, is a political contract between the States*; a national compact Or the word is applied to the agreement of the individuals of a community.
>
> The law of nations depends on mutual compacts, treaties, leagues, etc.

The above definition from Webster's 1828 dictionary explicitly mentions that the Constitution of the United States is a political **contract** between the States. This is supported by what has been covered so far:

- Unions (i.e., marriages, confederations, federations, associations, leagues, etc.) join two or more entities together in a binding relationship.
- Unions require that an implicit or explicit contract be established among the participating members.
- The union contract contains underlying articles,[4] laws, bylaws, or terms to set expectations and govern the intercourse between the union members.
- Articles, laws, bylaws, rules, and terms cannot be imposed upon the union members without their prior consent to be governed.
- The United States is a union that is currently made up of fifty States "united."
- The Constitution of the United States is the current-day political contract between the States.
- The Constitution's underlying Articles set expectations for the States and governs the mutual intercourse between them.

The Constitution is not a singular over-arching [statutory] law, but rather a contract that exists **only** among the State governments that comprise the Union. As the federal government is not a State, it is not a contracting party to the U.S. Constitution.

Because the States are the only parties to the Constitution, and

---

4 A single clause in a contract, account system of regulations, treaty, or other writing; a particular separate charge or item, in an account; a term, condition, or stipulation, in a contract.

because the States created the federal government, the conditions put forth in the Constitution's underlying Articles are directed towards States and federal governing bodies, not the private sector nor non-political entities. The Constitution is, therefore, a political document that only applies to civil governing bodies. The U.S. Constitution and the various State constitutions should be read from the perspective of what the federal government and the various State governments are explicitly permitted or forbidden to do.

Activating the Union Contract

Because a contract must be established before its underlying terms can become effective and enforceable, the U.S. Constitution (i.e., the States' contract) had to be established (ratified) before any of its underlying Articles could be enforced.

> U.S. Constitution (Article VII)
>
> The Ratification[5] of the Conventions of nine States, shall be sufficient for the Establishment of this Constitution between the States so ratifying the Same.

Per Article VII of the Constitution, the Union contract would be established after being ratified by nine States. Those States wishing to join the Union required approval from their citizens via the ratification process. Ratification is equivalent to willfully consenting to and "signing off" on the terms of the contract. Ratification initiated the process of the State entering into the Union. Delaware was the first State to ratify the contract and join the new federation union. The remaining

---

5 To confirm; to establish; to settle. To approve and sanction; to make valid; as, to ratify an agreement or treaty

50

forty-nine States subsequently joined the Union on the dates below, thereby entering into a political compact with the other States:

1. Delaware   December 7, 1787
2. Pennsylvania   December 12, 1787
3. New Jersey   December 18, 1787
4. Georgia   January 2, 1788
5. Connecticut   January 9, 1788
6. Massachusetts   February 6, 1788
7. Maryland   April 28, 1788
8. South Carolina   May 23, 1788
9. New Hampshire   June 21, 1788
10. Virginia   June 25, 1788
11. New York   July 26, 1788
12. North Carolina   November 21, 1789
13. Rhode Island   May 29, 1790
14. Vermont   March 4, 1791
15. Kentucky   June 1, 1792
16. Tennessee   June 1, 1796
17. Ohio   March 1, 1803
18. Louisiana   April 30, 1812
19. Indiana   December 11, 1816
20. Mississippi   December 10, 1817
21. Illinois   December 3, 1818
22. Alabama   December 14, 1819
23. Maine   March 15, 1820
24. Missouri   August 10, 1821
25. Arkansas   June 15, 1836
26. Michigan   January 26, 1837

27. Florida	March 3, 1845
28. Texas	December 29, 1845
29. Iowa	December 28, 1846
30. Wisconsin	May 29, 1848
31. California	September 9, 1850
32. Minnesota	May 11, 1858
33. Oregon	February 14, 1859
34. Kansas	January 29, 1861
35. West Virginia	June 20, 1863
36. Nevada	October 31, 1864
37. Nebraska	March 1, 1867
38. Colorado	August 1, 1876
39. North Dakota	November 2, 1889
40. South Dakota	November 2, 1889
41. Montana	November 8, 1889
42. Washington	November 11, 1889
43. Idaho	July 3, 1890
44. Wyoming	July 10, 1890
45. Utah	January 4, 1896
46. Oklahoma	November 16, 1907
47. New Mexico	January 6, 1912
48. Arizona	February 14, 1912
49. Alaska	January 3, 1959
50. Hawaii	August 21, 1959

Notice that there is no ratification date for the federal government. This is because the federal government is not a State and, therefore, cannot join the union. This also means that the federal government is not a member of the United States nor a contractual party to the Constitution.

The Supreme Law of the Land

I have covered some key concepts regarding contracts and unions, shared some key historical events, and briefly covered certain founding organic documents to support my argument that the U.S. Constitution is a contract rather than a law. However, Article VI of the Constitution might appear to contradict my position:

> <u>U.S. Constitution (Article VI)</u>
>
> This Constitution, and the Laws of the United States which shall be made in Pursuance thereof; and all Treaties made, or which shall be made, under the Authority of the United States, shall be the supreme Law of the Land; and the Judges in every State shall be bound thereby, any Thing in the Constitution or Laws of any State to the Contrary notwithstanding.

Webster's 1828 dictionary defines "law" as something that is "laid, set, or fixed, like statute, constitution." Statutory law and constitutional law are used as two examples of laws, but the terms are not mutually inclusive. The difference is that statutory law governs the populace while constitutional law governs the government. Statutory laws are those binding laws established by a legislative body that commands something on the populace or prohibits them from doing something. Regarding the Constitution, it is my position that Article VI's reference to "Law" was **not** intended to be statutory in its application, but rather a pronouncement for the purpose of regulating the behavior between the States. I will provide some basic points to support this position. The first point to consider is that Article VI groups the Constitution, the Laws of the United States, and Treaties as the "Law (singular reference) of the Land" rather than the "Laws (plural reference) of the Land." This collective grouping should bring the meaning of "Law" into question, considering that a treaty[6], by definition, is a **contract** established between two or more sovereign nations, countries, or States. For example, nations sometimes enter into a treaty to establish peace, establish commerce, or for creating military alliances. As previously mentioned, a document cannot primarily serve as both a contract and a law. It must be one or the other, as a contract and a law serve different purposes. If a treaty *were* a [statutory] law, then it should be expected that the Framers of the Constitution would have delegated treaty-making powers to the federal legislative branch of government, considering that the Constitution delegates all legislative powers of the union to the U.S. Congress:

U.S. Constitution (Article I, Section 1)

All legislative Powers herein granted shall be vested in a Congress of the United States, which shall consist of a Senate and House of Representatives.

It should be noted that the procedure to make treaties is listed within Article II, and such powers are vested within the president of the United States, by and with the advice and consent of only the Senate:

U.S. Constitution (Article II, Section 2)

He shall have Power, by and with the Advice and Consent of

6 An agreement, league or contract between two or more nations or sovereigns, formally signed by commissioners properly authorized, and solemnly ratified by the several sovereigns or the supreme power of each state. Treaties are of various kinds, as treaties for regulating commercial intercourse, treaties of alliance, offensive and defensive, treaties for hiring troops, treaties of peace, etc.

the Senate, to make Treaties, provided two thirds of the Senators present concur;

Per Article II, the federal Senate operates as an advising and consenting body (not a legislative one). Furthermore, the federal House of Representatives is excluded from the treaty-making process! This means that a treaty cannot be viewed as a statutory law, as law-making powers are vested fully in Congress. And if we **are** to purport that the Constitution and treaties are [statutory] laws, then we must also pose the question, "Why was Congress (i.e., the legislative branch) not delegated the necessary powers to alter them?" The above information requires that we re-examine the context of Law in relationship to other types of Laws that exist. Webster's 1828 dictionary provides a definition of **Law** (i.e., the Law of Nations) that would better support Article VI's verbiage and the relationship between the States of the union:

Laws of Nations

Laws of nations - the rules that regulate the mutual intercourse of nations or states. These rules depend on natural law or the principles of justice which spring from the social state; or they are founded on customs, compacts, treaties, leagues and agreements between independent communities.

By the law of nations, we are to understand that code of public instruction, which defines the rights and prescribes the duties of nations, in their intercourse with each other.

Considering what has been presented so far, I purport that "Law" refers to the "Laws of Nations." Based on natural law, the "Laws of Nations" is a prescribed code of conduct established and exercised between nations or States, in which each nation or State is expected to honor and abide by. Per the definition, the "Laws of Nations" are founded upon customs, compacts, treaties, leagues, and agreements established between independent communities. In the context of Article VI, "Law" would represent the Law [of Nations] code of conduct that governs the relationship that exists among the various States, and the code of conduct that would govern the relationship between the collective States (i.e., the United States) and other nations byway of treaties.

Recall that nations, countries, and States are sovereign and independent entities. Therefore, any treaty that the United States enters into with another nation is not legally enforceable, and any party to the treaty can technically breach the underlying terms at will. A governing body with the power to enforce international treaties does not currently exist. This means that the integrity of such treaties can only be maintained by a universal code of conduct respected and exercised by all parties. All parties to the treaty are expected to self-regulate their actions and intercourse with the other nations or States and honor the terms as if they were law. For this reason, the "supreme Law of the Land" should not be viewed as an overarching statutory law that governs over everybody and everything within the United States. Rather, it must be viewed as a natural law that requires each member State to adhere to the terms of their political contract - the Constitution of the United States - as a matter of honor and integrity. Another point that should make us question the meaning of "Law" in Article VI, as briefly mentioned earlier, is that the Framers (i.e., the delegates) of the Constitution were not delegated legislative powers to establish statutory law. Such powers must come directly from us (i.e., We, the People) through the election process. The delegates who attended the convention in Philadelphia were sent to represent their respective State's interests in the Union and to address certain flaws within the Articles of Confederation; thus, the delegates were granted the necessary powers to debate and negotiate the terms of the union contract. They did not attend for the purpose of establishing statutory law. If there was any expectation that the delegates would be meeting to establish a law that would govern everybody and everything in the "land," then each State surely would have sent an equal or greater number of delegates to the convention than the other States, to better their chances for more political representation in the union. However, this was not the case. Rhode Island did not send any delegates to the convention. The other twelve States sent a varying number of delegates to Philadelphia.

Lastly, a contract/agreement must precede a law or rule. Those who will be governed by the law must first consent to be governed and must delegate specific powers to the governing body. There must be an agreement between the governing and the governed. This is a fundamental principle of natural law, mentioned in the Declaration of Independence. So, if the Constitution is a law, then what founding document currently represents the preceding contract to the Constitution? There is none that exists.

Parties to the Union Contract

It has been shown that the "United States" is a political union among States, not a country. It has also been shown that the U.S. Constitution is a political contract between the States, not a law that governs all in the Land. Thus, it should be determined who is (and who is not) a member to the Union and a party to the contract.

The Federal Government

The Government of the United States (i.e., the federal government) is not a party to the U.S. Constitution, nor a member of the United States, because the federal government is not a State nor resides within a State. Technically, this means that any positions that fall under the umbrella of the federal government—such as federally elected positions and federal agencies—are *not* part of the United States. Therefore, in effect, they are not part of the Union. As revealed in the name, the Framers of the Constitution established a "Government of the United States" to externally and impartially govern the union (i.e., relationship) that existed among the member States. As such, it was never intended to become a State nor should be allowed to. As the federal government is not a State, it cannot join the United States. For this same reason, neither can the federal government become a party to the U.S. Constitution.

If this *were* allowed, it would create a conflict of interest between the federal government and the collective States, and compromise the federal government's impartiality to govern the union.

Washington D.C.

The U.S. Constitution specifies that a separate district (not exceeding ten square miles) be created and become the "Seat of the Government of the United States" (i.e., the Seat of the Federal Government):

> U.S. Constitution (Article I, Section 8)
>
> To exercise exclusive Legislation in all Cases whatsoever, over such District (not exceeding ten Miles square) as may, by Cession of particular States, and the Acceptance of Congress, become the Seat of the Government of the United States, and to exercise like Authority over all Places purchased by the Consent of the Legislature of the State in which the Same shall be, for the Erection of Forts, Magazines, Arsenals, dock-Yards, and other needful Buildings;

Article I, Section 8 is important because if the federal government were to preserve its impartiality as a neutral and impartial governing body of the union, its buildings and operations could not be physically located within the jurisdiction or territory of any given State. For this reason, Washington D.C. (District of Columbia) was carved out and became the "Seat of the Government of the United States." Given that Washington D.C. is not a State further supports the fact that the federal government is not a member of the United States nor a contracting party to the Constitution.

Territories of the United States

The territories of the United States are not States; therefore, they are not members of the United States nor parties to the U.S. Constitution. Rather, territories of the United States—as is evident in the name—are under the dominion of the collective member States. Since U.S. territories are not political parties to the U.S. Constitution, they are not required to adhere to its terms. Instead, territories are governed and regulated by the federal Congress:

> U.S. Constitution (Article IV, Section 3)
>
> The Congress shall have Power to dispose of and make all needful Rules and Regulations respecting the Territory or other Property belonging to the United States; and nothing in this Constitution shall be so construed as to Prejudice any Claims of the United States, or of any particular State.

If a U.S. territory wishes to join the United States, it must first become a State, then be admitted into the Union by the federal Congress. Only then does it become a member of the Union and an equal party to the Constitution of the United States:

> U.S. Constitution (Article IV, Section 3)
>
> New States may be admitted by the Congress into this Union; but no new State shall be formed or erected within the Jurisdiction of any other State; nor any State be formed by the Junction of two or more States, or Parts of States, without the Consent of the Legislatures of the States concerned as well as of the Congress.

We, the People

We the People are not members *to* the United States, but rather citizens *of* the States that, in turn, are members of the United States. This means that U.S. citizens are not a party to the Constitution. Recall: a constitution exists to establish a governing body and to delegate specific duties and powers to the government. It is a political document intended to govern political bodies; thus, the Articles and underlying verbiage of the U.S. Constitution are directed towards political institutions, not the private sector. We the People are not [technically] required to adhere to any of its Articles, nor are we required to adhere to any union laws established by the federal government. However, because the Constitution is currently [mis] interpreted as being a statutory law that "supremely governs all of the land," We the People have been compelled to adhere to its terms and federal laws. I purport that this was not the Framers' intention.

Amending the Union Contract

Because the Constitution is a contract, its contracting parties (i.e., the States) may find it necessary to alter its terms. Article V establishes the procedure for amending the contract:

> U.S. Constitution (Article V)
>
> The Congress, whenever two thirds of both Houses shall deem it necessary, shall propose Amendments to this Constitution, or, on the Application of the Legislatures of two thirds of the several States, shall call a Convention for proposing Amendments, which, in either Case, shall be valid to all Intents and Purposes, as Part of this Constitution, when ratified by the Legislatures of three fourths of the several States, or by Con-

ventions in three fourths thereof, as the one or the other Mode of Ratification may be proposed by the Congress; Provided that no Amendment which may be made prior to the Year One thousand eight hundred and eight shall in any Manner affect the first and fourth Clauses in the Ninth Section of the first Article; and that no State, without its Consent, shall be deprived of its equal Suffrage in the Senate.

Article V provides two methods for proposing Amendments:

1. Two-thirds of the federal congress is required to propose changes.
2. Two-thirds of the member States are required to call a convention for proposing changes.

Both methods require that three-fourths of the member States ratify the changes to amend the contract. Because the States are the only parties to the contract, they are the only ones authorized to approve proposed changes to the Constitution. This arrangement reinforces the concept that if the integrity of a contract is to be maintained, it may only be established, amended, or dissolved by the contracting parties. Notice that the federal government is not included in the amendment ratification process. This is because it is not a member of the United States nor a contracting party to the union contract. Furthermore, as U.S. territories are not States, they, too, are excluded from the ratification approval process. If the Constitution were a statutory law, it would be expected that Article V would have given the federal legislative body (i.e., the federal Congress) the power to alter it. Again, this would be especially true considering that Article I of the Constitution mentions that "All legislative Powers herein granted shall be vested in a Congress of the United States, which shall consist of a Senate and House of Representatives." However, the federal legislative body is not involved in the approval process. That power is solely reserved for the States.

There is a danger that comes with interpreting the Constitution as a law; when we believe something is a law, then we look to lawmakers to change the law. However, when we identify something as a contract, then we look to the contracting parties to amend the contract. Because we have [mis]identified the Constitution as being a law, the federal Congress has conveniently used its lawmaking powers in ways that have amended, overwritten, and negated parts of the States' contract. The federal government, established to enforce the union contract, has assumed certain powers reserved for the States.

The Union Flag

There have been two unions and three union contracts established by the various States since the original thirteen States declared their independence from the British Crown. The first union to be established was the "United States." The original thirteen States of the union entered into their first political contract under the Articles of Confederation (1777). The States later dissolved the Articles of Confederation and replaced it with their second union contract: The Constitution of the United States (1787).

The second union to be established was the "Confederate States of America," as a result of the Southern States seceding from the United States. The Southern States entered into a third political contract and compact under the "Constitution of the Confederate States of America (1861)." The current flag of the United States symbolically represents the thirteen States that established a confederation under the Articles of Confederation (first union contract) and that of the fifty States currently in a federation under the Constitution of the United States (second union contract). The original thirteen States are represented by the thirteen stripes on the current U.S. flag, while the fifty States are represented by the fifty stars.

The Bill of Rights

The first ten Amendments made to the union contract are collectively known as the "Bill of Rights." The Bill of Rights speaks to certain natural, civil, and legal rights guaranteed to the citizens of the Union. Many Americans misinterpret the Bill of Rights as the source of some of their rights, thinking that the Bill of Rights permissively grants certain rights to We, the People. However, a quick read will reveal that the Bill of Rights do not contain any permissive clauses. On the contrary, the Bill of Rights contains *prohibitive* clauses as a way to protect our inalienable rights from government infringement. This is supported by its preamble, which mentions that the Amendments are intended to place restrictions on the government:

Bill of Rights (Preamble)

The Conventions of a number of the States, having at the time of their adopting the Constitution, expressed a desire, in order to prevent misconstruction or abuse of its powers, that further declaratory and restrictive clauses should be added: And as extending the ground of public confidence in the Government, will best ensure the beneficent ends of its institution.

The Bill of Rights consists of restrictive clauses and words (e.g., prohibited, no, shall not) directed towards the government for the purpose of protecting our basic rights from government infringement.[1] The Amendments instruct the various governments as to what they must permit and what they are not allowed to do:

The First Amendment

Congress shall make no law respecting an establishment of religion, or prohibiting the free exercise thereof; or abridging the freedom of speech, or of the press; or the right of the people peaceably to assemble, and to petition the Government for a redress of grievances.

The First Amendment mentions that Congress *shall not establish... shall not prohibit... and shall not abridge* those rights listed in its verbiage. Again, *the First Amendment uses restrictive terms, not permissive ones.* The First Amendment prohibits Congress from using its legislative powers to limit or infringe upon the exercise of religious beliefs, free speech, freedom of the press, free assembly, or to petition the government for a redress of grievances.

The Second Amendment

A well regulated Militia being necessary to the security of a free State, the right of the people to keep and bear Arms[2], shall not be infringed.

---

1 To break; to violate; to transgress; to neglect to fulfill or obey; as, to infringe a law.
2 Weapons of offense, or armor for defense and protection of the body.

66

Note that the Second Amendment does not contain any permissive clauses that grants anyone the "right to bear arms." For example, it does not mention that "the people have the right" or "the people are permitted" or "the people are granted the right to bear arms." On the contrary, its verbiage is prohibitive: [such a right] "shall not be infringed." Thus, it is incorrect to believe or proclaim that it is your "Constitutional right to bear arms," as if the Constitution is the source of this right. If the Constitutional **had granted** this right, then the "right to bear arms" would be a government granted privilege rather than an inherited inalienable right.

The Bill of Rights was amended to the States' contract for the purpose of protecting our most sacred inalienable rights (e.g., religious liberty, freedom of speech, the right to bear arms), which are endowed to each individual by their Creator. Several State constitutions mention this self-evident truth:

Texas Constitution (Preamble)
Humbly invoking the blessings of Almighty God, the people of the State of Texas, do ordain and establish this Constitution.

(Article I. Bill of Rights, Section 2)
INHERENT POLITICAL POWER; REPUBLICAN FORM OF GOVERNMENT. All political power is inherent in the people, and all free governments are founded on their authority, and instituted for their benefit. The faith of the people of Texas stands pledged to the preservation of a republican form of government, and, subject to this limitation only, they have at all times the inalienable right to alter, reform or abolish their

government in such manner as they may think expedient.

Pennsylvania Constitution (Preamble)

WE, the people of the Commonwealth of Pennsylvania, grateful to Almighty God for the blessings of civil and religious liberty, and humbly invoking His guidance, do ordain and establish this Constitution.

Sec 1. Inherent rights of mankind.

All men are born equally free and independent, and have certain inherent and indefeasible rights, among which are those of enjoying and defending life and liberty, of acquiring, possessing and protecting property and reputation, and of pursuing their own happiness.

It should also be noted that "We the People" are not required to adhere to the Bill of Rights, as its Articles are aimed towards restricting government's authority; thus, private sector entities (i.e., businesses, organizations, citizens, etc.) are [technically] not required, for example, to accommodate or facilitate another individual's right to bear arms; or to exercise their freedom of speech or exercise their right to exercise certain religious liberties. For example, a business does not have to permit the exercise of religious freedoms within their work environment; a homeowner does not have to allow free speech within their home; an organization does not have to permit peaceful assembly within its purview. However, it should be understood that individuals and businesses *cannot* encroach upon the inalienable rights of others if such rights are being exercised outside the individual's or business's personal property boundary lines. For example, a business owner cannot infringe upon someone's inalienable rights if that person is exercising such rights *external* to the business owner's property lines or purview.

The Government of the United States

"The powers delegated by the proposed Constitution to the federal government are few and defined. Those which are to remain in the State governments are numerous and indefinite."
— *James Madison, Federalist 45, 1788*

I would like to briefly cover the federal government's role and its relationship to the United States and to the U.S. Constitution. Recall that the federal[1] government—referenced as the **"Government of the United States"** in the Constitution—is an external governing body to the Union and, therefore, is **not** a member of the United States. Recall, it is only the actual States that are united. The primary function of the Government of the United States, as revealed in the name, is to govern the "United States." That is to say, its purpose is to govern the relationship that exists among the States. It must be emphasized that the federal government governs the *relationship* that exists between the States; it was not delegated any powers to govern

---

1 Pertaining to a league or contract; derived from an agreement or covenant between parties, particularly between nations.

Consisting in a compact between parties, particularly and chiefly between states or nations; founded on alliance by contract or mutual agreement; as a federal government, such as that of the United States.

Leagued; united by compact, as sovereignties, states or nations; joined in confederacy; as federate nations or powers.

over the States themselves, nor to govern the citizens within each State. Furthermore, the federal government was not delegated any powers to govern or regulate private sector entities. Such powers are reserved for the States, specifically granted to each State by its citizens through State Constitutions. As an example, the Homeowners Association Governing Board exists to govern the relationship that exists among the homeowners of the neighborhood. The HOA governing board does not have authority to govern over the homes, the homeowners themselves, nor over individuals who resides within the home. The individual homeowners retain the sole discretion of governing themselves and their household. A federal government that governs the affairs of the member States—or the affairs of their respective citizens, which is currently the case—violates the intent of State independence and individual liberty. It is precisely because the federal government was established to *serve* the States that its delegated powers were designated as "few and defined"—a way to protect State independence. The enumerated powers delegated to each of the federal branches are listed in the Constitution. The legislative powers are vested in the federal Congress; the executive powers are vested in the president; the judicial power is vested in the Supreme Court.

The Federal Congress

Congress - The assembly of senators and representatives of the several states of North America, according to the present constitution, or political compact, by which they are united in a federal republic; the legislature of the United States, consisting of two houses, a senate and a house of representatives. Members of the senate are elected for six years, but the members of the house of representatives are chosen for two years only. Hence the united body of senators and representatives for the two years, during which the representatives hold their seats is called one congress. Thus we say the first or second session of the sixteenth congress.

The above definition supports what has already been presented: that the several States are united in a federal republic[2], and the States of the union physically reside on the [North] American continent. The federal congress, comprised of the Senate and House of Representatives, is the legislative body of the Union. The States delegated specific and limited powers to the legislative branch for the purpose of enacting certain laws that would better govern the relationship that exists between the individual States and govern the relationship between the union and foreign nations. To reiterate, the U.S. Constitution does not delegate any powers to the federal congress to make laws that govern individuals or businesses that exist within the private sector. Any current federal law that govern businesses or individuals are assumed powers which violate the States' contract. Article I of the Union contract lists the bulk of those responsibilities and powers delegated to the federal Congress.

Article I, Section 1

All legislative Powers herein granted shall be vested in a Congress of the United States, which shall consist of a Senate and House of Representatives.

---

2 A commonwealth; a state in which the exercise of the sovereign power is lodged in representatives elected by the people. In modern usage, it differs from a democracy or democratic state, in which the people exercise the powers of sovereignty in person. Yet the democracies of Greece are often called republics.

72

The Federal Executive

The federal executive[3] branch is the law-enforcing branch of the Union. Per its name, the executive branch's primary duty is to "execute" (to carry into effect) and enforce the underlying Articles with the union contract, and those union laws enacted by the federal Congress. The federal executive branch is also responsible for protecting the union from internal and external threats. Because the executive branch at the various levels of government is responsible for law enforcement and protection, it possesses the weaponry required to support its duties. Article II contains most of the duties delegated to the federal executive branch. The president of the union is the chief executive officer for the executive branch.

The President of the United States

The office of the presidency[4] is one of the most misunderstood positions within the federal government. This is not because the Framers were vague or misleading in their description of the office and its duties. Rather, it is primarily because recent generations have been indoctrinated to believe that the President of the United States (POTUS) holds the highest political position; that he is the designated leader of the "country"; that he is responsible for setting an agenda for "America"; and that he governs over the entire "country" and runs the federal government—none of which is true. As

---

3 Having the quality of executing or performing; as executive power or authority; an executive officer. Hence, in government, executive is used in distinction from legislative and judicial. The body that deliberates and enacts laws, is legislative; the body that judges, or applies the laws to particular cases, is judicial; the body or person who carries the laws into effect, or superintends the enforcement of them, is executive.

4 An officer appointed or elected to govern a province or territory, or to administer the government of a nation. The president of the United States is the chief executive magistrate.

the name suggests, presidents do ***preside*** over things. For example, the president of a company presides over the company and governs its affairs, concerns, and helps to maintain order. However, the president (whomever that may be at any given time) does ***not*** preside over the individual lives and affairs of the employees. The president only has authority over the positions within the company but does not have authority over the individuals within those positions. In the context of the U.S. Constitution, the "President of the United States" presides over the United States. However, it is important to recall that the United States is a union (i.e., a type of relationship), not a country. Thus, the President of the United States presides over the intangible ***relationship*** that exists among the States, but was not delegated any powers to preside over the affairs of the States themselves, nor preside over the affairs of the individuals that reside within the various States. This is why it is important to stop referencing the "United States" as a country, as it gives the impression that the President of the United States presides over a whole country, which is not the case. As previously revealed, the "United States" is the given name of the union between the states:

Articles of Confederation (Article I)
The Stile of this confederacy shall be, "The United States of America."

The President of the United States is the chief executive magistrate of the union. The executive branch at all levels of government is responsible for enacting and enforcing those laws established by the legislative branch. As part of the federal executive branch, it is the president's job to execute (i.e., carry out) and enforce the laws of the union and the Articles within the States' contract (the U.S. Constitution). That is to say, the president's primary role is that of a contract enforcer. The president takes an oath to this effect:

<u>U.S. Constitution (Article II, Section 1)</u>
Before he enter on the Execution of his Office, he shall take the following Oath or Affirmation: "I do solemnly swear (or affirm) that I will faithfully execute the Office of President of the United States, and will to the best of my Ability, preserve, protect and defend the Constitution of the United States."

Recall, the collective States **created** the federal government (i.e., legislative, executive, and judicial branches) as a byproduct of the Constitution being ratified. It should be emphasized that we (human beings) create things to serve us, not for us to serve our creations. Thus, the intent was for the federal government (the creation) to serve the States (its creators), not for the States to serve the federal government. As part of the federal government, the office of the presidency was created for the purpose of **serving** the States by preserving, protecting, defending, and enforcing the terms of their political contract (i.e., the Constitution of the United States). In so doing, he protects the integrity of the contract and the Union itself. It should be emphasized that there is nothing in the president's inaugural oath that explicitly states or suggests that the president's job is to lead the nation, rule over the States, fix the economy, improve public education, or establish policies that govern the private sector. The office of the presidency, being a **creation** of the States, was established as a position of servitude, not one of leadership. Furthermore, recall that the federal government (which includes the POTUS) is an *external* governing body to the United States. Its delegated powers were established by the States to be limited rather than broad, which should negate the belief that the president's role is to lead the nation.

It is critical to reiterate that the POTUS does not preside over the States (nor their respective citizens) any more than the president of an HOA presides over the homeowners or those who reside within their household. Article II of the Constitution lists most of the executive branch's delegated powers. Because the POTUS presides over the union that exists among the States, he or she is to report to Congress on the state (i.e., condition or welfare) of their union from time to time.

> Article II, Section 3
>
> He shall from time to time give to the Congress Information of the State of the Union, and recommend to their Consideration such Measures as he shall judge necessary and expedient; he may, on extraordinary Occasions, convene both Houses, or either of them, and in Case of Disagreement between them, with Respect to the Time of Adjournment, he may adjourn them to such Time as he shall think proper; he shall receive Ambassadors and other public Ministers; he shall take Care that the Laws be faithfully executed, and shall Commission all the Officers of the United States.

Article II, Section 3 of the U.S. Constitution mentions that the president shall from time to time give the Congress information on the "state of the Union." Notice there is no mention of the "state of the Country." The purpose behind the "state of the union" address would probably be better understood if renamed the "Condition of the Relationship between the States" address.

The Federal Judiciary

Article III of the States' contract is relatively short. It delegates specific and limited powers to the Union's supreme Court. The supreme Court *serves* the States by [impartially] adjudicating over conflicts that arise between the member States. Article III mentions that the judicial power of the United States shall be vested in one supreme Court, and in such inferior Courts as the Congress may from time to time ordain and establish. However, "supreme" does not mean that the supreme Court's adjudication powers are supreme over **all** things. Like its sister branches, the supreme Court's powers are limited, not broad. Article III of the Constitution explicitly mentions those cases and controversies over which the supreme Court jurisdiction reigns supreme:

Article III, Section 2

The judicial Power shall extend to all Cases, in Law and Equity, arising under this Constitution, the Laws of the United States, and Treaties made, or which shall be made, under their Authority; - to all Cases affecting Ambassadors, other public Ministers and Consuls; - to all Cases of admiralty and maritime Jurisdiction; - to Controversies to which the United States shall be a Party; - to Controversies between two or more States; - between a State and Citizens of another State, - between Citizens of different States, - between Citizens of the same State claiming Lands under Grants of different States, and between a State, or the Citizens thereof, and foreign States, Citizens or Subjects.

It is understandable that those who have adopted the perspective that the United States is a country would be prone to conclude that the Supreme Court is the highest court in the country. However, this viewpoint would place the Supreme Court's powers above the powers vested in the Supreme Courts of the States, which was not the Framers' intention.

The supreme Court is the highest court in the Union. Thus, Article III extends the supreme Court jurisdiction over the controversies that may arise between two or more member States of the union. It does not extend the Supreme Court powers over the States themselves. Any conflict that arises within a State and does not conflict with the terms within the States' contract, are to be adjudicated by that respective State's supreme Court only. Because the supreme Court serves the States, its authoritative hierarchal position is also beneath the States. Using a homeowners' association as an example, whenever two or more homeowners have a dispute, an external and impartial governing body (i.e., the HOA governing board) is needed to adjudicate the conflict. To do so, the HOA governing board must have "supreme" authority over the dispute, as the other homeowners lack the authority and the impartiality to adjudicate the matter. The HOA governing board, established to *serve* the homeowners, has jurisdiction only over the conflict that may arise between two or more homeowners, not over the homeowners themselves. This premise applies to the federal supreme Court as well; thus, the supreme Court is not supposed to strike down a State law just because other States disagree with the law. If a State law does not violate the Union contract or Union laws, the Supreme Court [technically] has no judicial authority over the matter. The law in question becomes a State matter, to be addressed by the State constitution, its government, its Supreme Court, or its citizens.

Non-enforcement of the Union contract

The States established the federal government to serve the States by enforcing the States' contract, establishing certain laws that would better the mutual intercourse among the States, and to adjudicate conflicts that may arise between two or more member States. Because the Constitution is a political contract between the States, each of the member States has the responsibility and the right (i.e., just claim) to protect its interests, its citizens, and its sovereignty if the federal government fails, neglects, or refuses to perform its delegated duties. This is not to suggest that the States take immediate action on day one of a federal government failure; rather, it emphasizes the natural premise that once a delegated duty is neglected, the duty and its associated responsibility reverts back to the delegator, at which point the delegators can either perform the duty themselves or re-assign it to another delegate. This principle, founded upon the Laws of Nature, is endorsed within the Declaration of Independence:

> That whenever any Form of Government becomes destructive of these ends, it is the Right of the People to alter or to abolish it, and to institute new Government, laying its foundation on such principles and organizing its powers in such form, as to them shall seem most likely to effect their Safety and Happiness -- this same principle applies to the States as well.

State Secession

Secede - To withdraw from fellowship, communion or association; to separate ones' self; as, certain ministers seceded from the church of Scotland about the year 1733.

The Southern Confederacy

Many Americans are familiar with the history surrounding the Southern States seceding from the Union. It remains a sore spot in American history. However, I believe it is important to address the subject as a way to provide a historical example that emphasizes the two primary points made in this book: that the United States is a Union, and that the Constitution of the United States represents the union contract. I do not intend to [personally] argue the justification for the Southern States' choice to secede, but rather show why *they* believed that they had the justified right to do so.

First, it is important to recall that the United States is a union, not a country; thus, it is incorrect to say, "the Southern States seceded from the country or split the country in half." As the United States is a union comprised of several independent and sovereign States, each State has the right (i.e., just claim) to "divorce" and separate itself from the Union. Because each State willfully acceded into the

Union, each can willfully secede from it. That is to say, members of any type of union, league, confederation, or association can willfully withdraw from their relationship just as they willfully joined it. This is a matter of natural principle. A spouse who willfully enters into a marital union has the right to willfully divorce from it. A recent example of this principle may be seen in the United Kingdom: as a nation, they willfully chose to enter into the European Union, and later willfully voted to exit the Union in 2016 (a decision known as Brexit). All persons, organizations, and countries have the natural right to separate from anything deemed detrimental or disadvantageous to their existence, happiness, or well-being. Such was the case with the Southern States: each individual State chose willfully to accede into the United States and each one later chose to willfully secede from the United States. Each of the Southern States who seceded issued an "Ordinance of Secession," formally dissolving their political relationship with those States that remained members of the United States. In so doing, the Southern States exercised their sovereign right to secede from one union (i.e., the United States of America) and then chose to establish another. The Southern States named their new union the "Confederate States of America," a name which confirmed that there were now *two* distinct and separate political unions that resided on the continent of [North] America. Secession from the United States also meant that the Southern States were no longer contracting parties to the previous union contract (i.e., the Constitution of the United States); thus, they were no longer bound to adhere to any of the Articles within the U.S. Constitution. Nor were they subject to any federal laws enacted under the United States, as the Government of the United States (i.e., the federal government) had been established to govern only the United States of America, of which they were no longer a part—not the Confederate States of America.

The Southern States' new union contract (i.e., the Constitution of the Confederate States, 1861) contained Articles that would govern their new union. Similar to the U.S. Constitution, the preamble of the Confederate Constitution mentioned that each member State of the Union had the right to act in its sovereign and independent character:

> Constitution of the Confederate States (Preamble)
> We, the people of the Confederate States, each State acting in its sovereign and independent character, in order to form a permanent federal government, establish justice, insure domestic tranquility, and secure the blessings of liberty to ourselves and our posterity invoking the favor and guidance of Almighty God do ordain and establish this Constitution for the Confederate States of America.

Upon secession, the Confederate States created their own union, independent and separate from the United States. In so doing, they also established another political contract—the third union contract to be established among the several States since their declared independence from Great Britain.

Just as the Southern States willfully joined the Union, they had the right, as an independent body politic, to secede from the Union. Negative consequences may arise from such a choice—to secede from a union—but such consequences do not negate one's right to do so. The Southern States did not break any laws by making this choice, as no law existed that prohibited them from doing so. Parties to a union, regardless of type, must consent to choosing to unite, but do not require permission from the other members if they choose to withdraw. By definition, any union that prohibits its members from willfully leaving cannot be considered a union; thus, the Southern States were not obliged to ask permission from the federal government or any other State when they deemed it necessary to dissolve their relationship with the United States of America.

Conclusion

In this treatise, I have presented information to support my position that the Constitution is a political contract and not a law. I would like to sum up the main points that support this actuality:

- The "United States" is the given name of the union that exists among the current fifty States. The United States is not a country.
- The United States, as evidenced by its name, is comprised of States, united.
- The union that exists among the States physically resides on the continent of "America;" hence, the "United States of America."
- The members of all unions, regardless of the type of union, engage with each other according to the terms and laws of a binding contract designed and intended to govern the relationship among the union members.
- A contract must precede any laws that will govern the contracting parties.
- The "Constitution of the United States" is the current political contract that exists between the fifty member States of the Union. The federal government is not a State; thus,

it is not a member of the United States nor a contracting party to the U.S. Constitution.

- The Articles within the Constitution exist to regulate the mutual intercourse between the member States, and to delegate specific powers to the "Government of the United States" (i.e., the federal government).

- The States created the Government of the United States to serve several purposes: 1) to establish certain laws that would govern and better the relationship among the States, 2) to enforce the union laws and terms of the States' political contract, and 3) to adjudicate disputes that might arise between the States.

Contracts and Laws (regardless of type) serve different purposes, so it is important that we correctly identify what the U.S. Constitution is at its core. This idea may seem insignificant to most, but the correct interpretation will allow us to protect our liberties and inalienable rights, and more accurately understand our system of government, rather than what we believe it to be.

Appendix

1828 Webster's Dictionary Definitions

Alliance

1. The relation or union between families, contracted by marriage.

2. The union between nations, contracted by compact, treaty or league.

3. The treaty, league, or compact, which is the instrument of confederacy; sometimes perhaps the act of confederating.

4. Any union or connection of interests between persons, families, states or corporations; as, an alliance between church and state.

Amendment

1. An alteration or change for the better; correction of a fault or faults; reformation of life, by quitting vices.

America

One of the great continents, first discovered by Sebastian Cabot, June 11, O.S. 1498, and by Columbus, or Christoval Colon, Aug. 1, the same year. It extends from the eightieth degree of North, to the fifty-fourth degree of South Latitude; and from the thirty-fifth to the one hundred and fifty-sixth degree of Longitude West from Greenwich, being about nine thousand miles in length. Its breadth at Darien is narrowed to about forty-five miles, but at the northern extremity is nearly four thousand miles. From Darien to the North, the continent is called North *america* and to the South, it is called South *america*

Arms

1. Weapons of offense, or armor for defense and protection of the body.

Article

1. A single clause in a contract, account system of regulations, treaty, or other writing; a particular separate charge or item, in an account; a term, condition, or stipulation, in a contract. In short, a distinct part of a writing, instrument or discourse, consisting of two or more particulars; as, articles of agreement; an account consisting of many articles.

Bill

14. A bill of rights is a summary of rights and privileges, claimed by a people. Such was the declaration presented by the lords and commons of England to the prince and princess of Orange in 1688. In America, a bill or declaration or rights is prefixed to most of the constitutions of the several states.

Declaration

1. An affirmation; an open expression of facts or opinions; verbal utterance; as, he declared his sentiments, and I rely on his declaration

2. Expression of facts, opinions, promises, predictions, etc., in writings; records or reports of what has been declared or uttered.

4. A public annunciation; proclamation; as the declaration of Independence, July 4, 1776.

Delegate

1. A person appointed and sent by another with powers to transact business as his representative; a deputy; a commissioner; a vicar. In the United States, a person elected or appointed to represent a state or a district, in the Congress, or in a Convention for forming or altering a constitution.

Charter

1. A written instrument, executed with usual forms, given as evidence of a grant, contract, or whatever is done between man and man. In its more usual sense, it is the instrument of a grant conferring powers, rights and privileges, either from a king or other sovereign power, or from a private person, as a charter of exemption, that no person shall be empannelled on a jury, a charter of pardon, etc. The charters under which most of the colonies in America were settled, were given by the king of England, and incorporated certain persons, with powers to hold the lands granted, to establish a government, and make laws for their own regulation. These were called charter-governments.

Citizen

1. The native of a city, or an inhabitant who enjoys the freedom and privileges of the city in which he resides; the freeman of a city, as distinguished from a foreigner, or one not entitled to its franchises.

5. In the United States, a person, native or naturalized, who has the privilege of exercising the elective franchise, or the qualifications which enable him to vote for rulers, and to purchase and hold real estate.

Clause

2. An article in a contract or other writing; a distinct part of a contract, will, agreement, charter, commission, or other writing; a distinct stipulation, condition, proviso, grant, covenant, etc.

Common Law

In Great Britain and the United States, the unwritten law, the law that receives its binding force from immemorial usage and universal reception, in distinction from the written or statute law. That body of rules, principles and customs which have been received from our ancestors, and by which courts have been governed in their judicial decisions. The evidence of this law is to be found in the reports of those decisions, and the records of the courts. Some of these rules may have originated in edicts or statutes which are now lost, or in the terms and conditions of particular grants or charters; but it is most probable that many of them originated in judicial decisions founded on natural justice and equity, or on local customs.

Compact

An agreement;

a contract between parties; a word that may be applied, in a general sense, to any covenant or contract between individuals; but it is more generally applied to agreements between nations and states, as treaties and confederacies. So the constitution of the United States is a political contract between the States; a national *compact* Or the word is applied to the agreement of the individuals of a community.

The law of nations depends on mutual compacts, treaties, leagues, etc.

Confederate

To unite in a league; to join in a mutual contract or covenant.

By words men come to know one another's minds; by these they covenant and confederate

The colonies of America confederated in 1775.

Several States of Europe have sometimes confederated for mutual safety.

Confederation

1. The act of confederating; a league; a compact for mutual support; alliance; particularly of princes, nations or states.

The three princes enter into a strict league and *confederation*

2. The United States of America are sometimes called the *confederation*

Congress

1. A meeting of individuals; an assembly of envoys, commissioners, deputies, etc., particularly a meeting of the representatives of several courts, to concert measures for their common good, or to adjust their mutual concerns.

2. The assembly of delegates of the several British Colonies in America, which united to resist the claims of Great Britain in 1774, and which declared the colonies independent.

3. The assembly of the delegates of the several United States, after the declaration of Independence, and until the adoption of the present constitution, and the organization of the government in 1789. During these periods, the congress consisted of one house only.

4. The assembly of senators and representatives of the several states of North America, according to the present constitution, or political compact, by which they are united in a federal republic; the legislature of the United States, consisting of two houses, a senate and a house of representatives. Members of the senate are elected for six years, but the members of the house of representatives are chosen for two years only. Hence the united body of senators and representatives for the two years, during which the representatives hold their seats is called one congress Thus we say the first or second session of the sixteenth congress

Continental

Pertaining or relating to a continent; as the continental powers of Europe. In America, pertaining to the United States, as continental money, in distinction from what pertains to the separate states; a word much used during the revolution.

Constitution

4. The established form of government in a state, kingdom or country; a system of fundamental rules, principles and ordinances for the government of a state or nation. In free states, the *constitution* is paramount to the statutes or laws enacted by the legislature, limiting and controlling its power; and in the United States, the legislature is created, and its powers designated, by the *constitution*

Contract

1. An agreement or covenant between two or more persons, in which each party binds himself to do or forbear some act, and each acquires a right to what the other promises; a mutual promise upon lawful consideration or promise upon lawful consideration or cause, which binds the parties to a performance; a bargain; a compact. Contracts are executory or executed.

Convention

3. An assembly. In this sense, the word includes any formal meeting or collection of men for civil or ecclesiastical purposes; particularly an assembly of delegates or representatives for consultation on important concerns, civil, political or ecclesiastical. In Great Britain, convention is the name given to an extraordinary assembly of the estates of the realm, held without the kings writ; as the assembly which restored Charles II. to the throne, and that which declared the throne to be abdicated by James II. In the United States, this name is given to the assembly of representatives which forms a constitution of

92

government, or political association; as the convention which formed the constitution of the United States in 1787.

Country

2. The whole territory of a kingdom or state, as opposed to city. We say, the gentleman has a seat in the *country* at any distance from town indefinitely.

3. Any tract of land, or inhabited land; any region, as distinguished from other regions; a kingdom, state or lesser district. We speak of all the countries of Europe or Asia.

Delegate

1. A person appointed and sent by another with powers to transact business as his representative; a deputy; a commissioner; a vicar. In the United States, a person elected or appointed to represent a state or a district, in the Congress, or in a Convention for forming or altering a constitution.

Executive

Having the quality of executing or performing; as executive power or authority; an executive officer. Hence, in government, executive is used in distinction from legislative and judicial. The body that deliberates and enacts laws, is legislative; the body that judges, or applies the laws to particular cases, is judicial; the body or person who carries the laws into effect, or superintends the enforcement of them, is executive.

Federal

1. Pertaining to a league or contract; derived from an agreement or covenant between parties, particularly between nations.

2. Consisting in a compact between parties, particularly and chiefly between states or nations; founded on alliance by contract or mutual agreement; as a federal government, such as that of the United States.

3. Friendly to the constitution of the United States.

Flag

An ensign or colors; a cloth on which are usually painted or wrought certain figures, and borne on a staff. In the army, a banner by which one regiment is distinguished from another. In the marine, a banner or standard by which the ships of one nation are distinguished from those of another, or by which an admiral is distinguished from other ships of his squadron. In the British navy, an admiral's flag is displayed at the main-top-gallant-mast-head, a vice-admiral's at the fore-top-gallant-mast-head, and a rear-admiral's at the mizen-top-gallant-mast-head.

Governor

1. One who is invested with supreme authority to administer or enforce the laws; the supreme executive magistrate of a state, community, corporation or post. Thus, in America, each state has its governor; Canada has its *governor*

Immigration

The passing or removing into a country for the purpose of permanent residence.

94

Intercourse

1. Communication; commerce; connection by reciprocal dealings between persons or nations, either in common affairs and civilities, in trade, or correspondence by letters. We have an intercourse with neighbors and friends in mutual visits and in social concerns; nations and individuals have intercourse with foreign nations or individuals by an interchange of commodities, by purchase and sale, by treaties, contracts, etc.

Infringe

1. To break, as contracts; to violate, either positively by contravention, or negatively by non-fulfillment or neglect of performance. A prince or a private person infringes an agreement or covenant by neglecting to perform its conditions, as well as by doing what is stipulated not to be done.
2. To break; to violate; to transgress; to neglect to fulfill or obey; as, to infringe a law.

Land

2. Any portion of the solid, superficial part of the globe, whether a kingdom or country, or a particular region. The United States is denominated the land of freedom.

Leader

1. One that leads or conducts; a guide; a conductor.
2. A chief; a commander; a captain.
3. One who goes first.

Marriage

The act of uniting a man and woman for life; wedlock; the legal union of a man and woman for life. marriage is a contract both civil and religious, by which the parties engage to live together in mutual affection and fidelity, till death shall separate them. marriage was instituted by God himself for the purpose of preventing the promiscuous intercourse of the sexes, for promoting domestic felicity, and for securing the maintenance and education of children

Nation [to be born]

1. A body of people inhabiting the same country, or united under the same sovereign or government; as the English nation; the French nation It often happens that many nations are subject to one government; in which case, the word nation usually denotes a body of people speaking the same language, or a body that has formerly been under a distinct government, but has been conquered, or incorporated with a larger nation…

Naturalization

The act of investing an alien with the rights and privileges of a native subject or citizen. *naturalization* in Great Britain is only by act of parliament. In the United States, it is by act of Congress, vesting certain tribunals with the power.

Party

3. One concerned or interested in an affair. This man was not a *party* to the trespass or affray. He is not a *party* to the contract or agreement.

President

2. An officer appointed or elected to govern a province or territory, or to administer the government of a nation. The president of the United States is the chief executive magistrate.

Ratify

2. To approve and sanction; to make valid; as, to *ratify* an agreement or treaty.

Secede

To withdraw from fellowship, communion or association

Sovereign

1. Supreme in power; possessing supreme dominion; as a *sovereign* ruler of the universe.

State

5. A political body, or body politic; the whole body of people united under one government, whatever may be the form of the government.

Municipal law is a rule of conduct prescribed by the supreme power in a *state*

More usually the word signifies a political body governed by representatives; a commonwealth; as the States of Greece; the States of America. In this sense, *state* has sometimes more immediate reference to the government, sometimes to the people or community. Thus when we say, the *state* has made provision for the paupers, the word has reference to the government or legislature; but when we say, the *state* is taxed to support paupers, the word refers to the whole people or community.

Stile

[This is another spelling of style. See Style and Still.]

Supreme

1. Highest in authority; holding the highest place in government or power. In the United States, the congress is supreme in regulating commerce and in making war and peace. The parliament of Great Britain is supreme in legislation; but the king is supreme in the administration of the government. In the universe, God only is the supreme ruler and judge. His commands are supreme, and binding on all his creatures.

Territory

1. The extent or compass of land within the bounds or belonging to the jurisdiction of any state, city or other body.
2. A tract of land belonging to and under the dominion of a prince or state, lying at a distance from the parent country or from the seat of government; as the territories of the East India Company; the territories of the United States; the territory of Michigan; Northwest territory These districts of country, when received into the union and acknowledged to be states, lose the appellation of territory

Treaty

1. An agreement, league or contract between two or more nations or sovereigns, formally signed by commissioners properly

authorized, and solemnly ratified by the several sovereigns or the supreme power of each state. Treaties are of various kinds, as treaties for regulating commercial intercourse, treaties of alliance, offensive and defensive, treaties for hiring troops, treaties of peace, etc.

Union

1. The act of joining two or more things into one, and thus forming a compound body or a mixture; or the junction or coalition of things thus united. *union* differs from connection, as it implies the bodies to be in contact, without an intervening body; whereas things may be connected by the intervention of a third body, as by a cord or chain.

7. States united. Thus the United States of America are sometimes call the *union*

Unite

1. To put together or join two or more things, which make one compound or mixture. Thus we unite the parts of a building to make one structure. The kingdoms of England, Scotland and Ireland united, form one empire. So we unite spirit and water and other liquors. We unite strands to make a rope. The states of North America united, form one nation.

2. To join; to connect in a near relation or alliance; as, to unite families by marriage; to unite nations by treaty.

Usurp

To seize and hold in possession by force or without right; as, to usurp a throne; to usurp the prerogatives of the crown; to usurp power. To usurp the right of a patron, is to oust or dispossess him.

Welfare

2. Exemption from any unusual evil or calamity; the enjoyment of peace and prosperity, or the ordinary blessings of society and civil government; applied to states.

www.ingramcontent.com/pod-product-compliance
Lightning Source LLC
Chambersburg PA
CBHW022059210326

41520CB00046B/732